MEG and MOG SHOW

Book, music and lyrics by
David Wood

Based on Meg and Mog books
by Helen Nicoll and
Jan Pieńkowski

Samuel French – London
New York – Sydney – Toronto – Hollywood

ISBN 978-0-573-05065-7

www.samuelfrench-london.co.uk

www.samuelfrench.com

MEG AND MOG SHOW was originally commissioned by Unicorn Theatre, and produced by them at the Arts Theatre, London, on 10th December 1981, with the following cast of characters:

Meg	Maureen Lipman
Mog	Vincent Osborne
Owl	Carrie Simcocks
Stegosaurus	Ben Robertson
Tess	Pamela Power
Jess	Tim Bannerman
Cress	Andrew Sargent
Bess	Mary Roscoe
Sir George	Ben Robertson
Sir François	Tim Bannerman
Zookeeper	Andrew Sargent
Tiger	Tim Bannerman
Astronaut	Pamela Power

Directed by Tony Wredden and David Wood
Designed by Jan Pieńkowski with Vikie Le Saché
Lighting designed by Angus Stewart

Music arranged and directed by Peter Pontzen
Magic Adviser The Great Kovari
Choreography by Pamela Power

Day Trip to the Moon sung by Julia McKenzie with Libby Ritchie

ACT I

Scene 1	Meg's Home
Scene 2	Meg's Kitchen
Scene 2a	The Flight to the Witches
Scene 3	Hilltop. The Witches' Spell Party
Scene 4	The Castle
Scene 5	The Zoo

ACT II

Scene 1	The Zoo
Scene 1a	The Flight to the Moon
Scene 2	The Moon
Scene 2a	The Flight Home
Scene 3	Meg's Garden

The Meg and Mog books, by Helen Nicoll and Jan Pieńkowski, upon which *Meg and Mog Show* is based are:

Meg and Mog
Meg's Eggs
Meg on the Moon
Meg's Castle
Mog at the Zoo

published by William Heinemann.

The photographs in this text are from the original productions by Unicorn Theatre at the Arts Theatre, London and are by Donald Cooper and Laurence Burns.

CHARACTERS

MEG—a Witch, whose spells often go wrong
MOG—her Cat; because he is mute, he has to communicate with mime
OWL—her pet Owl; he can hoot, and uses the "oo" sound to suit every occasion
STEGOSAURUS—a prehistoric monster, which grows extra segments during the play; these segments can be played by actors pantomime horse-style
TESS
JESS
CRESS
BESS
} the Witches
SIR GEORGE—a peace-loving knight with a lisp
GHOST 1
GHOST 2
SIR FRANÇOIS—a large war-loving knight of French extraction
ZOOKEEPER—possibly with a regional accent
TIGER—elderly, of impeccable Indian Raj background
ASTRONAUT

It is possible for four actors to play all the parts other than Meg, Mog and Owl. However, in the original production it was found that using five was more practical.

These four or five could also be involved in the suggested "black theatre" and puppetry sequences.

It is also possible, in a school production, for example, to increase the cast by adding animals in the zoo scene or by stretching the Stegosaurus. A choir could provide support in some of the songs, and be featured in the song *Day Trip to the Moon.*

SONGS

ACT I

1	MEG, MOG AND OWL	Meg, (Mog), Owl
2	STEGGY STEGOSAURUS	Stegosaurus
3	WHICH WITCH IS WHICH?	Meg, Bess, Tess, Jess, Cress
4	THE SPELL	Bess, Tess, Jess, Cress
5	TO THE ZOO	Meg, (Mog), Owl, Sir George

ACT II

6	LONG IN THE TOOTH	Tiger (Meg and Owl as optional chorus)
7	DAY TRIP TO THE MOON	Off-Stage or pre-recorded voices
7A	STEGGY STEGOSAURUS (*reprise*)	Stegosaurus
8	LULLABY	Owl (plus Meg and Audience)
8A	THE SPELL (*reprise*)	Meg
8B	TO THE ZOO (*reprise*)	Zookeeper, Meg, (Mog), Owl, Stegosaurus
9	I GOT A SPELL RIGHT	Meg, (Mog), Owl, Tess, Jess, Cress, Bess
9A	I GOT A SPELL RIGHT/ MEG, MOG AND OWL (*reprise*)	Meg, (Mog), Owl, Tess, Bess, Jess, Cress

The piano/vocal score is available from Samuel French Ltd.

AUTHOR'S NOTE

Meg and Mog Show is an adaptation of five of a series of books by Helen Nicoll and Jan Pieńkowski. These books are very popular with young children at school and at home. The economy of language is useful for early reading and the stories lend themselves to imaginative discussion and creative learning. The characters are particularly appealing. I hope very much that the show is faithful to the books. The characters have adapted, I believe, very successfully to the three dimensional stage and the situations they get into encourage audience participation and involvement. The majority of children in the audience will be acquainted with the books and their distinctive style. I believe that both directors and designers would profit from referring to the books for guidance, both for sets and costumes. Jan Pieńkowski's use of colour is particularly distinctive and most effective dramatically as well as on the printed page. It is also possible that children would be disappointed if their favourite characters did not resemble the picture books they know and love. They are published in hardback by Heinemann and paperback by Puffin. Those relevant to this show are: *Meg and Mog, Meg's Eggs, Meg on the Moon, Meg's Castle* and *Mog at the Zoo*. The basic staging of the show should be quite straightforward. However, there are several challenges to designers and directors. These involve flying. Meg, Mog and Owl use this mode of travel, sometimes on a broomstick and once inside a cauldron. The methods used in the original production are described in this Acting Edition. Other productions, depending on the technical facilities available, may discover other methods, whether simpler or more sophisticated.

David Wood

DESIGN NOTES by Jan Pieńkowski

The bold style of the Meg and Mog books can be interpreted for the design of the show to produce an effect of great clarity and humour.

The World of Meg and Mog

Three black and white characters live in a bright uncluttered world of strong shapes and primary colours. Few things are patterned or shaded and each setting is suggested with the minimum of means. The keynote of the design is economy.

Style
If in doubt—leave it out. As in the books, the sets should be as simple as possible. Simplicity in the design adds to the comedy and makes impossible things appear quite matter of fact.

Shadow puppets
These sequences achieve the impossible—i.e. the flight of the characters in the most simple way. The small black silhouettes, so instantly recognizable from the Meg and Mog books, make excellent links.

Props
The broomstick and cauldron would both naturally be black, but to show up against black backgrounds the cauldron can be liberally covered with glitter and the broomstick sprayed silver. The cauldron's "window highlight" also helps.

The cauldron is best made of strong foam with removable bottom and large enough for all three characters to get inside.

All the "magic" props should be very big and bright and U.V. if possible.

The moon buggy can be adapted from a bicycle or supermarket trolley and the rocket is flat.

Costumes
The principals are all in black and white.

MEG Her shoes are the most important single item—worth spending a lot of your design budget on—make them comfortable but spectacular. Dress should be very short with long points, and zig-zag sleeves. Hair can be enhanced with string or raffia.

MOG Black leotard with white furry "doughnut" stripes and sprung, spiral tail. He has yellow eyes—otherwise he is black, an excellent part for a black actor.

OWL In contrast, a white ball of feathers, with white fluffy fur, tights and big round spectacles.

STEGOSAURUS Green with pink spots.

TIGER Yellow and black striped combinations.

FOUR WITCHES All in black with as much variety of size and shape as possible. To emphasize Meg's distinctive appearance the other witches would do well to have long skirts and domestic brooms.

KNIGHTS Red and white tunic with silver armour for Sir George and black and yellow for Sir François with hobby horses to match. The "armour" can be very effectively suggested by household utensils, e.g. dustbin lids, colanders and baking trays.

ZOOKEEPER Blue uniform, wellingtons, apron.

Sets
Clean, strong shapes in flat strong colours work best. Primary colours are used in all the books as a foil to the black and white characters. All the pieces are flat, even the bed, and primary coloured cloths provide a variety of backgrounds.

Design problems
The magic sequences involving black theatre tend to make Meg, Mog and the Witches disappear. Glitter fabric and silver spray are the best solution.

Carrie Simcocks as OWL, Amanda Barrie as MEG, TIM Bannerman as TIGER and Vincent Osborne as MOG

Maureen Lipman as MEG

Ben Robertson as
SIR GEORGE

Amanda Barrie as MEG

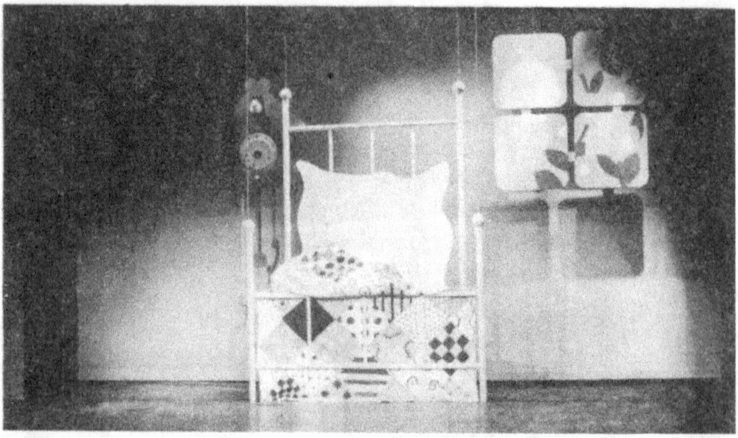

Act 1 Scene 1

Act 1 Scene 4

Act II Scene 2

Shadow puppets as designed by Jan Pieńkowski for the original Unicorn Theatre production

ACT I

Scene 1

Meg's Home

It is suggested that this scene is performed against a red backcloth. A cut-out window with four window panes hangs in front. A green cuckoo clock with telephone receivers as "weights" stands next to the bed in which Meg, Mog and Owl are discovered sleeping. This bed is a cut-out, in which the three actors can stand, *thus being more visible to all the audience than if they were lying down. The pillow, against which we see their heads, should be white. The bed is covered with a quilt*

As the curtain rises, two noises are heard—the "tick tock" of the cuckoo clock (attached to one side of the bed) and the contented snores and whistling hoots of the sleeping Meg and Owl. Mog is hidden under the quilt

Meg (Snore)
Owl Ooooo!
Meg (Snore)
Owl Ooooo!
Meg (Snore)
Owl Ooooo!

Suddenly the alarm bell rings violently. Meg, Mog and Owl do not react at first. But eventually Meg, who is in the middle, stretches out an arm to press the "off" knob under the face of the clock. She misses, and presses Owl's nose instead. A hooter effect is heard. Owl reacts with a muffled hoot, and, waking up, rubs his nose. He is mystified, not knowing how his nose got pressed. The alarm bell continues to ring as Owl settles to sleep again. A second time, Meg's hand reaches out and by mistake presses Owl's nose. Hooter. Owl reacts as before. The third time, Owl wakes up properly and realises what is going on. He switches off the alarm clock, looks over at the snoozing Meg and Mog, scratches his head, and takes a deep breath, then hoots at Meg, trying to wake her up

Owl Whoo! Whoo! Whoo!

The third hoot is loud enough to wake Meg up, with a jump. She looks about, blinking, and sees Owl

Meg Morning, Owl.
Owl Whoo!

Meg (*looking at the clock*) Is that the time? That clock. It never rings. Never ever.

Owl (*trying to point out that it* did *ring*) Whoo! Whoo!

Meg Exactly. What's the use of an alarm clock that doesn't alarm? I'll mend it. By magic.

Owl (*nervously*) Ooh!

Music as Meg "fluences" the clock and incants the spell. Owl shields his eyes, nervous. The light pulsates magically

Meg
I charm this clock
This alarmless clock
This useless thing
I command to ring!

The clock face turns into the dial of a telephone which rings loudly

Oh dear. I didn't mean that

Owl answers the phone, by picking up one of the "weights"

Owl Whoo! (*Meaning "hello"*) Who? Oo! (*Handing it to Meg*) Oo! (*Meaning "it's for you"*)

Meg (*putting the receiver to her ear*) Hallo. Meg here.

Telephone (*politely*) Good morning. This is your alarm call.

Meg How kind.

Telephone (*rudely*) Get up!

Meg How rude.

Meg throws the receiver to Owl, who replaces it

(*Calling*) Mog! Where's Mog?

Owl (*indicating*) Whoo!

Meg (*seeing him*) Morning, Mog. Catnap over! Time to get up.

Mog emerges, making himself visible for the first time. He does a wild, yawning stretch and retreats further beneath the bedclothes

Mog!

SONG 1: MEG, MOG AND OWL

Meg (*introducing herself and her friends*)
Meg, Mog and Owl

Owl Whoo!

Meg Owl

Owl Whoo!

Meg
Mog and Meg
It's getting late
It's half past eight
Time for us to shake a leg.

Music continues as Meg and Owl get out of bed, stretch, and maybe do the odd exercise or dance

Meg Meg, Mog and Owl

Meg notices that Mog is still asleep—Owl uses his hoot to try to wake him up

Owl Whoo!
Meg Owl
Owl Whoo!
Meg Meg and Mog
(*Speaking*) Mog!
He's still asleep
I'll make him leap—
(*In Mog's ear*) Mog, look out—here comes a dog! (*She barks*)

Mog leaps out of bed and crouches warily

(*Speaking*) It's all right, Mog. I was only joking! (*She strokes Mog*)

First a Witch!
Second a Bird!
Owl Whoo!
Meg Third
A Cat who can't say a word!

Through thick or thin
Owl Whoo!
Meg Fair
Owl Whoo!
Meg Wind or foul
Such friends as we
You'll seldom see—
Meg
Mog
And Owl!
Owl Whoo!

Meg (*speaking*) Dressing time!

The music continues as the dressing begins

Shoes!

Mog and Owl collect one shoe each from behind or in front of the bed. They display the shoes to Meg, who nods approvingly, then to the audience. Mog and Owl kneel, then lower their heads in order to put the shoes on Meg's feet. Their heads clash. They rub them. They try again. Their heads clash again. They rub them again. Meg tries to make things easier for them

(*To Owl, pointing at her left foot*) Left shoe!

Owl takes Meg's left leg

(*To Mog, pointing to her right foot*) Right shoe!

Mog takes Meg's right leg

Meg loses her balance and ends up on the floor. She waves Mog and Owl away

Cloak!

Mog and Owl return to the bed to find the cloak. Meg, meanwhile, has to put her shoes on herself. Mog and Owl return with the cloak and help Meg to put it on. Ideally this should be in an amusing way, putting it on back to front or over her head

Meg (*to Owl*) Hat! (*To Mog*) Broomstick!

Mog and Owl move together. Mog returns first with the broomstick and hands it to Meg. She transfers it to her other hand while checking her cloak. Owl returns with her hat, and places it on the end of the broomstick. Meg turns, sees her hat, and jumps with surprise. Mog puts the hat on Meg's head

Thank you.

The three present themselves to the Audience

Meg (*singing*) Owl
Owl Whoo!
Meg Mog
And
Meg!

Mog and Owl both mime hunger. Meg notices

What is it? What's the matter? (*To the Audience*) What's the matter with them? Does anybody know?
Audience They're hungry.
Meg They're what?
Audience Hungry.
Meg Hungry. (*To Mog and Owl*) Are you hungry?

They nod. Meg thinks

So am I. It's time for breakfast.

Mog and Owl react pleased

Downstairs!

Music, as Meg, carrying her broomstick, leads Mog and Owl off

SCENE 2

Meg's Kitchen

The bedroom set flies out, to reveal a yellow staircase against a black backcloth. Meg's cauldron is upstage. The black backcloth enables certain magical "black theatre" effects to be employed. Actors or Stagehands, dressed all in black, can be made invisible against a black background

Music as Meg, Mog and Owl enter, coming down the stairs into the kitchen

Meg Halt!

Mog and Owl concertina into Meg

Breakfast. Where's my cauldron?

Mog indicates it, and all three approach. Meg indicates to Mog and Owl to stand clear as she puts down her broomstick and prepares to do magic

Right. Breakfast spell.

As Meg calls out the ingredients, she, Mog and Owl produce them magically. The "black theatre" principle can be employed here. Each ingredient can "float" on, attached to a black rod

(*In a mysterioso voice*) Mix with a spider

A spider appears. Owl pops it in the cauldron

A nuthatch's nest

A nest appears magically. Mog pops it in the cauldron

Add a squashed beetle

A beetle appears magically and is put in the cauldron

And hope for the best.

(*Whispering*) Broomstick.

Mog hands Meg the broomstick. Meg waves it over the cauldron

Abracadabra
Riddle me ree
By the power of my broomstick
Bring breakfast for three!

There is a flash and a puff of smoke. Black-out

It's working!

Extraordinary noises

The lights come up again to reveal, in the cauldron, Stegosaurus. (*In the original production, Stegosaurus entered the cauldron during the black-out through the black curtains behind it. It was found that this could be done very speedily*)

Aaaah! I must have added too much beetle.

Owl (*nervously*) Whoo! Whoo!

Meg You're not our breakfast.

Stegosaurus No. You're *my* breakfast! (*He roars threateningly and pounds his chest*)

Meg What? You can't eat us!

Stegosaurus I can! (*He steps out of the cauldron and advances downstage*)

Meg Who do you think you are?

Stegosaurus I'm Stegosaurus.

Meg Steggy who?
Stegosaurus Stegosaurus.
Meg Well, we wanted an eggy, not a Steggy.

SONG 2: STEGGY STEGOSAURUS

During the song, Stegosaurus threatens Meg, Mog and Owl. Towards the end of the first verse, he grabs Meg's broomstick from her, and tries to eat it

Stegosaurus Yummy yummy yum
I'm a
Steggy Stegosaurus
Ug ug yummy
I'm a
Steggy Stegosaurus
Fill my tummy
I'm a prehistoric beast
And I'm greedy for a feast
Where's my breakfast?

He can't eat the broomstick, so snaps it in two, and throws down the pieces

Yummy yummy yummy
Scrummy scrummy scrummy
Chewy gooey chewy
Slurp! (*noise*)

He snatches Meg's hat and tries to eat it

Munchy munchy munchy
Scrunchy scrunchy scrunchy
Icky licky icky sticky
Burp! (*noise*)

He can't eat Meg's hat and throws it away. Meg catches it and puts it back on

Yummy yummy yummy
Scrummy scrummy scrummy
Chewy gooey chewy
Suck! (*noise*)

He grabs hold of Mog's tail and tries to eat it

Munchy munchy munchy
Scrunchy scrunchy scrunchy
Icky licky icky sticky
Yuck! (*noise*)

He throws Mog's tail back

During the rest of the song he looks around for food, and stalks Meg, Mog and Owl

I'm a
Steggy Stegosaurus

Ug ug yummy
I'm a
Steggy Stegosaurus
Fill my tummy
I'm a prehistoric beast
And I'm greedy for a feast
Where's my breakfast?
Yummy yummy
Yeah yeah yummy
Where's my breakfast?
Yummy yummy
Yeah yeah yummy
Where's my breakfast?
Oh where?

He carries on grunting and dashing around as Meg, Mog and Owl flap their arms and wings to try to get rid of him

Yummy! yummy!
Meg } (*together*) { Shoo! Shoo!
Owl } { Whoo! Whoo!
Stegosaurus Where's my breakfast? Yummy! Yummy!
Meg } (*together*) { Shoo! Shoo!
Owl } { Whoo! Whoo!
Stegosaurus Where's my breakfast?

Stegosaurus advances on Mog, who sidesteps neatly

Stegosaurus keeps going—off stage

Meg Well done, Mog. He's gone.

They congratulate each other

He's gone in the garden. He's . . .

An immediate loud crunching and biting sound stops them from relaxing. They rush to the side of the stage and look off

Owl (*alarmed*) Whoo! Whoo!
Meg (*with a gasp*) . . . he's gone in my cabbage patch!

The noises of munching get worse

(*Calling*) Hey, Steggy! You can't eat my cabbages!

The eating noise increases

Come here this second!

Immediately Stegosaurus returns

He knocks over Meg, Mog and Owl and charges round eating a large cabbage

Stegosaurus Munchy, munchy, crunchy, crunchy . . .

He dashes off again

Mog and Owl help Meg up. They look off again. The eating noises return

Meg He's pinching me parsnips now! (*Calling*) Stop it! Stop it! And hands off me hollyhocks!

Owl Whoo! Whoo!

Meg Exactly! Whoo! Whoo! What are we going to do, do? He's leeking off me polish!

Mog and Owl look at her

Owl Whoo?

Meg I mean he's polishing off me leeks. (*With a gasp*) And gobbling all me goosegogs!

Suddenly Stegosaurus returns, clutching a large leek. He knocks over Meg, Mog and Owl

Stegosaurus Yummy, yummy, scrummy, scrummy, slurp, slurp . . .

Meg, Mog and Owl get up, only to be knocked over again as Stegosaurus exits

Meg (*struggling up*) Oh no. Our beautiful garden. He'll ruin it.

Mog nudges Meg to gain her attention. The eating noises continue in the background

What?

Mog mimes "make a spell"

Make a magic spell? I've just made a magic spell, haven't I? And it all went wrong. *We* should be eating our breakfast now, not him.

Mog mimes again, "make a spell to get rid of him". Owl joins in

Owl Shoo! Shoo!

Meg Make a spell to get rid of him? But I don't know a getting-rid-of-Steggy spell. I didn't even know I knew a making-Steggy-*appear* spell.

The eating noises get louder

Suddenly, Stegosaurus, clutching a carrot, enters. He is visibly larger than last time he entered. (*In the original production a segment was added, pantomime horse-style*)

Stegosaurus pushes past Meg, Mog and Owl, knocking them over. Meg recovers, turns, sees Stegosaurus and screams

Aaaah! It's grown a thingy!

Meg faints into Mog's arms

Owl grabs the broom end of the broken broomstick and uses it as a fan to revive Meg

Mog succeeds in pushing Stegosaurus off

Meg revives

Quick. Mog's right. We need a spell. Before he eats *everything*! He might even eat us! We'll go and see the other witches and buy a spell from them. Broomstick!

Owl, rather ashamed, shows her the broken broomstick

That's no use. Where's the spare?

Mog indicates "upstairs"

Upstairs?

Mog nods and starts to go. Meg stops him

I'll get it.

She adopts her spell-chanting position

Music

Hocus pocus, it's no jokus
Broomstick number one is brokus
Broomstick two wake up, I cry
Downstairs I command you FLY!

Meg, Mog and Owl look off up the stairs

Whooshing noise of approaching broomstick. It flies in (black theatre principle), and excitedly jigs about; but it has flown in the side opposite the stairs and is therefore unseen by Meg, Mog and Owl

The Audience may shout out that the broomstick has arrived, but in any event, Mog notices it and indicates to the others, who turn and see it

Good.

She goes to take it, but it escapes her grasp and hovers provocatively. She grasps again

Come here!

But it jumps away again

And again

Come *here*!

She makes a dive for it, and it leaps in the air and hovers over her head

Where are you? Come here!

Mog and Owl point to it. Meg stretches for it, but it evades her, and in turn tickles Meg, Mog and Owl

Meg finally catches the broomstick and holds it horizontally in front of her

Right. Mog! Owl!

Mog and Owl join her. Meg and Mog hold the broomstick along its length. Owl watches.

All aboard! One, two, three, hup!

Meg and Mog each swing a leg over the broomstick, as though to sit on it. As they do so, the broomstick escapes, flies away a few feet and hovers. Meg and Mog sit on nothing and crash to the floor

(*Getting up*) Broomstick, behave! (*She grabs it as before*) All aboard!

Meg and Mog hold the broomstick

One, two, three, hup!

They swing a leg over. The broomstick escapes again. Meg and Mog fall to the floor

The broomstick hovers nearby, shaking

Where is it?

Mog and Owl indicate

Owl Whoo!

Meg sees it

Meg It's laughing at us, look. You cheeky stick, I'll make you shake with something else! Come here. Here!

Meg grabs the broomstick. She and Mog climb aboard again

All aboard. One, two, three, hup!

They are on

They're always the same, spare broomsticks. They're so seldom used that when they *are*, they get over-excited and show off. (*To Mog and Owl*) Ready?

She concentrates. Music

(*Beginning the spell*) Broomstick. I . . .

Mog suddenly interrupts her with a tap on the shoulder

What is it, Mog?

Mog points to the cauldron

The cauldron? What about it?

Mog mimes "take it with us"

Take it with us? Good idea.

Mog goes and fetches the cauldron. Holding on to its handle, he sits on the broomstick again

Ready?

Meg concentrates. Music

(*Beginning the spell*) Broomstick I . . .
Owl (*interrupting*) Whoo!
Meg (*annoyed*) What is it, Owl?

Owl exits

The broomstick moves in sharp bursts, like a bucking bronco. Meg and Mog react

(*Calling off to Owl*) Quick! The broomstick's frisky!

Owl dashes back with a package, plus a white cloth

What's that? Your sandwiches?
Owl Whoo! (*He nods and shows Meg the cloth*)
Meg And a tablecloth?

Owl nods, then puts the sandwiches on the cloth

To eat your sandwiches on?

Owl nods, and puts the sandwiches and the cloth in the cauldron

We're not going on a picnic, you know. Ready? (*She concentrates*)

Music

(*Chanting*) Broomstick I command you fly
Up to the witches in the sky!

Whooshing noise as the broomstick takes off

Black-out

Scene 2A

The Flight to the Witches

Music

A scene using shadow puppets on rods

In the original production a screen was incorporated into the front cloth. This flew in at the end of the previous scene, and the shadow puppets appeared almost immediately

It is suggested that the voices in the following shadow play section are voice-overs, preferably pre-recorded

Meg and Mog enter, on the broomstick, the cauldron hanging from the back. Owl flies behind. They enter DL *of screen and fly diagonally upwards*

Owl lags behind a little

Meg Keep up, Owl!

Owl catches up

All are now centre screen

Suddenly Meg's broomstick bucks and rears

Wayhay! This spare broomstick's still frisky! (*To broomstick*) Calm down!

The broomstick calms. All exit UR *of screen*

The lighting changes to blue, to suggest night

Jess enters on her broomstick from UR, *whirling and swooping, towards* DL

When nearly there . . .

Jess (*eerie and echoing*) Hallo!

Jess leads Tess (on her broomstick) in from DL

Tess Hallo!
Jess Follow! Follow!

They fly towards UR

Cress (on her broomstick) enters UR *and gracefully swoops down and up between Jess and Tess*

Cress Wheeeeeeeeeee! Hallo!
Tess
Jess } (*together*) Hallo!

Tess and Cress circle

Jess picks up Bess (on her broomstick) DL

Jess Follow! Follow!
Bess (*as she enters*) Hallo!

Jess leads Bess to the others

They line up in formation

Tess Ready to land!
All (*voices overlapping*) Land! Land! Land! Land! (*Together*) Wheeeee!

There is a "whooshing" sound effect as they all fly UR *and off*

Meg, Mog and Owl enter DL *and fly to centre*

Meg Look! There they are!

The Witches enter one by one from UR

Each Witch nearly collides with Meg, Mog and Owl. Meg tries to control her frisky broomstick

Witch 1 Hey! Watch out! (*She avoids them by going* over *them*)
Witch 2 Mind where you're flying! (*She avoids them by going* under *them*)
Witch 3 Get out of my flight path! (*She avoids them by going* over *them*)

Witch 4 Sky hog! (*She avoids them by going* under *them*)

Meg and Mog suddenly fly up; the broomstick is virtually out of control. Owl follows

Meanwhile the Witches form up under *them*

Meg Broomstick, behave!

Another "whooshing" sound effect, as Meg, Mog and Owl suddenly drop, scattering the Witches

Witches Aaaaaaaaaaah!
Meg Sorry!

Meg, Mog and Owl hover DC. *The Witches form up* above

Another "whooshing" sound effect as Meg, Mog and Owl rise, *scattering the Witches out of frame in an upward direction*

Witches Aaaaaaaaaaaaah!

Meg, Mog and Owl hover UC *then drop straight down, off screen*

Meg Oh! Oh! Ohhhhhhhhhhhh!

Black-out

A descending "whoosh" followed by a loud crash

Scene 3

Hilltop. The Witches' Spell Party

As quickly as possible, the lights go up to reveal that Meg, Mog and Owl have crash-landed. Timing is important. The shadow puppets in the previous scene should fall out of frame, the crash sounds should be heard during the black-out, and the screen should fly out to reveal Meg, Mog and Owl immediately afterwards

The scene can be played against a bare background—possibly dark blue—with a crescent moon and stars. A tree upstage

Meg, Mog and Owl roll on the ground, following the landing, then start to pick themselves up

One by one, the four Witches arrive. All should be immediately recognisable traditional witches, but should look a little different from each other, with individual witch-like characteristics

Tess enters, as though landing, accompanied by a "whooshing" noise

Tess Have you a licence to ride that thing?
Meg Yes, Bess.
Tess Bess?
Meg Yes.

Tess I'm Tess.
Meg Sorry, Tess.

Cress enters, as if landing, accompanied by a "whooshing" noise

Cress Disgraceful exhibition. Careering through the sky with no thought for other riders.
Meg Sorry, Jess.
Cress Jess?
Meg Yes.
Cress I'm Cress.
Meg Sorry, Cress. It's my spare broomstick. I'm running it in.

Jess enters, as if landing, accompanied by a "whooshing" noise

Jess You nearly ran it in to us!
Meg Sorry, Tess.
Jess Tess?
Meg Yes.
Jess I'm Jess.

Bess enters, as if landing, accompanied by a "whooshing" noise

Bess Are you insured to carry passengers?
Tess And luggage?
Cress Are you moving covens or something?
Jess I couldn't believe my eyes. I said to the others, "She's brought everything except the kitchen cauldron".
Tess
Bess } (*together*) And *we* said, "look, she's brought that as well!"
Cress

They cackle with laughter. Meg joins in, then checks herself

Meg I'm sorry, (*pointing, hesitatingly, at Bess*) Tess . . .
Bess Bess.
Meg (*pointing at Cress*) Jess.
Cress Cress.
Meg (*pointing at Tess*) Bess.
Tess Tess.
Meg (*pointing at Jess*) Cress.
Jess Jess.
Meg I'm sorry.
All 4 It's rude to call witches other witches' names.
Meg But . . .

SONG 3: WHICH WITCH IS WHICH

Meg (*speaking*) Which witch is which?
They all look the same
(*singing*) Which witch is which?
And which witch has which name?

Which witch is which?
Which witch are you?
I wish I could distinguish
Which witch is who!

Witches Which witch is which?
We all look the same
Which witch is which?
And which witch has which name?

Tess (*speaking*) Listen . . .
(*singing*) I'm Tess
Bess I'm Bess
Cress I'm Cress
Jess I'm Jess
Meg (*to Tess*) You're Bess?
Tess I'm Tess
Meg (*to Cress*) You're Jess?
Cress I'm Cress
Jess *I'm* Jess
Tess I'm Tess
Bess I'm Bess
Cress I'm Cress
Meg I must confess
I'm in a mess.

All Which witch is which?
We/they all look the same
Which witch is which?
And which witch has which name?

Witches Now Jess is less like Cress than Tess
And Bess is less like Tess than Jess
But Cress is less like Jess than Bess
Which witch is which?
Meg I still can't guess.

All Which witch is which?
We/they all look the same
Which witch is which?
And which witch has which name?

Bess
Tess } (*together*) The dresses of Jess and Cress
Need a press

Jess and Cress look annoyed

Jess
Cress } (*together*) The tresses of Bess and Tess
Look a mess

The Witches start arguing

Meg (*speaking*) Ladies! Please!

The Witches stop arguing and cackle

Witches (*speaking*) Ladies! Ha, ha, ha!
Tess (*singing*) I'm Tess
Meg You're Tess
Bess I'm Bess
Meg You're Bess
Cress I'm Cress
Meg You're Cress
Jess I'm Jess
Meg You're Jess
(*getting it right*) You're Tess, you're Bess, you're Cress, you're Jess.
Tess Yes
Bess Yes
Cress Yes
Jess Yes!
All Four Witches What a success!
You know
Which witch is which
Though we all look the same
You know
Which witch is which
And which witch has which name
You know
Which witch is which
And which witch is who—
So now
You'd better tell us
Which witch are *you!*

Meg (*speaking*) I'm Meg.
Tess Oh, it's Meg.
Bess No wonder, then.
Jess Always gets things wrong, Meg does.
Cress A disgrace to her profession.
Tess Well, now you're here, you'd better make yourself comfortable.
Meg Thank you . . . er, Tess?
Tess Yes. Witches' brew?
Meg Pardon?
Tess Would you care for some witches' special brew?
Meg Oh. Thank you.

Music

A magical sequence, during which Meg is provided with "Witches' brew". It is suggested that Tess is in charge of this demonstration, stage-managing the various tricks. It is further suggested that a magical adviser may well have ideas slightly different from the following routine. For instance, the teapot may be produced in a different manner. The main sequence of the routine, however, should be preserved

Tess takes off her hat (or the hat of another Witch), makes a magical pass over it and produces a white cup and saucer (stuck together), which she hands to Meg

Jess takes off her hat, makes a magical pass over it and produces a white teapot. She pours the Witches' brew into the cup

Cress takes off her hat, makes a magical pass over it and produces a milk bottle. She pours in the milk. Or she produces a rubber glove, blows it up and "milks" the fingers

Bess Sugar?
Meg Please.

Bess holds her clenched fist above the cup and saucer, and makes a magical pass over it. Sugar streams from her fist into the cup

Cress makes a magical pass and produces a spoon. She stirs Meg's brew, then makes the spoon disappear

The Witches indicate to Meg that she should try the brew. Meg drinks approvingly

Thank you.

The Witches cheer

(*Beckoning Mog and Owl*) This is my cat, Mog, and my owl, Owl.

The Witches "mm" approvingly

Jess Splendid specimens.

The Witches surround and examine Mog and Owl, who react embarrassed, not too sure whether they like it

Cress Are they for sale?
Meg Certainly not. I mean . . . they're my friends.
Cress Shame.
Bess How did you know we were having a Spell Party?
Meg Spell Party? Is this a Spell Party?
Bess I've just said so, stupid.
Meg Good. We've come to ask you for a spell.
Tess You want us to *sell* you a spell?
Meg Well, yes.
Jess Why didn't you say so before?
Cress We'll demonstrate some for you.
Bess Then you can choose one.

They excitedly turn away in order to prepare their spell show

Meg Ah. But we need a special spell.

The Witches gasp and turn back to Meg

Tess *All* our spells are special, my dear.
Jess Special . . .

Cress Spectacular . . .
Bess Splendiferous!
Meg But . . .

A big fanfare heralds the start of the "show". The Witches "place" their audience. Meg is unable to explain that they require a special spell to get rid of Stegosaurus

Each Witch in turn makes a spell, muttering beneath her breath, and performs a magic trick. Dialogue should be kept to the minimum—in other words "silent" tricks will be better than "patter" tricks. The Witches applaud each other and help each other as necessary

A magic adviser should assist the four Witches by finding suitable tricks that they can perform well. If possible, the tricks should relate in some way to the Witches and their surroundings. Each trick should not take too long. *If necessary, one trick could be performed by two Witches*

SUGGESTIONS

(*1*) *Mog is reluctantly inveigled into assisting a Witch, who causes his tail to visibly tie a knot in itself and then untie itself*

(*2*) *The dancing broomstick—an adaptation of the "dancing cane" effect*

(*3*) *A magical "production" from Meg's cauldron perhaps*

(*4*) *The "levitation" of Owl*

(*5*) *A disappearance trick—Owl or Mog could be made to disappear (using a trap is possible), then reappear from offstage. The Witches' cloaks could be useful for concealing Owl or Mog before "vanishing" them*

(*6*) *A trick using fire—a dove or flower production from a flaming "dove pan", perhaps?*

After the four Witches have each performed, they come to Meg eagerly

Tess Well?
Meg Well . . .
Jess Any spell you fancy?
Meg Well . . .
Cress You didn't like our spells?
Meg Oh yes, but . . .
Bess No buts. Special offer. Three spells for the price of two.
Meg You don't understand. A spell went wrong . . .
Tess How dare you!
Jess Our spells . . .
Cress . . . never . . .
Bess . . . go wrong.
Meg Not one of yours. One of mine.
Tess That's nothing new.
Jess Typical.
Cress It was a miracle you ever passed your magic exams . . .

Meg Please . . . listen!
Bess No, *you* listen. Then you might learn to get a spell right for once.
Meg (*in despair*) Mog, you tell them . . .

Mog scratches his head, then launches into a mime. The Witches interpret it

Mog points to Meg

Tess Meg . . .

Mog mimes doing a spell

Jess Did a spell . . .

Mog pats his stomach

Cress And made you ill . . .

Mog shakes his head and mimes eating

Bess A food spell?

Mog nods

Mm. Tricky, food spells.

Mog mimes (*using the cauldron*) *Stegosaurus emerging from the cauldron*

Tess A monster. She made a monster?

Mog nods

Jess What sort of monster?

Mog scratches his head, sees the Audience and mimes for help from them. Cress picks this up

Cress (*nervously, to the Audience*) What sort of monster?
Audience A Stegosaurus.
Cress A what?
Audience A Stegosaurus.
All Four Witches (*in horror*) A STEGOSAURUS?
Meg (*recovering*) Yes. And it's eating everything in the garden, and growing and growing and growing.
Bess Why didn't you tell us before?
Meg I tried to . . . please, you must help us.
Tess This is serious. We need a head to head.

The Witches get together in a sort of rugger scrum, and circling, mutter unintelligible murmurings

Finally they straighten

Jess We are agreed.
Cress You need a . . .
All Four Witches Getting-rid-of-Stegosaurus spell!
Meg We know that. Can you give us one?
All Four Witches Give?

Meg Well, sell.
All Four Witches Mmm.

They get back down into their "head to head". More muttering

Finally . . .

Bess We are agreed.
Tess Listen . . .

SONG 4: THE SPELL

Bess, Tess, Jess and Cress
Take a red ostrich feather
And mix it together
With the tooth of a tiger—sharp and white
Then add a cup of moondust—sparkling bright
Stir the ingredients, stir them well
Close your eyes and whisper this secret spell—

The next two lines could be divided up to give clarity to each ingredient

Feather, tooth, moondust
Tickle, bite, sneeze
Be gone Stegosaurus
Gone with the breeze.

Meg Oh thank you. (*She repeats the words of the spell to help her remember it*)

Feather, tooth, moondust
Tickle, bite, sneeze
Be gone Stegosaurus
Gone with the breeze.

All Four Witches Yes!
Bess First you must find the three ingredients.
Meg Yes, of course. Thank you, witches.
All Four Witches Your pleasure is our reward. (*They stretch out their hands*) And our reward is your pleasure!
Meg Yes, of course. What can I give you?
Tess Your cat?
Jess Your owl?
Cress Your broomstick?
Bess Your cauldron?
Meg Oh no, please. I'll never be a proper witch without them.
Cress You'll never be a proper witch until you get your spells right.
All Four Witches (*in sharp agreement*) Mm!
Meg I tell you what. Let me find the three ingredients, get rid of Steggy, and prove to you I can get a spell right. Then you can all come to my garden for a Spell Party to celebrate. All right?
All Four Witches (*after a pause*) All right.
Meg Good. Now, we must be off. First ingredient. An ostrich feather.

Bess A *red* ostrich feather.
Meg Mmm. Where on earth can we find a red ostrich?
Tess We'll give you a spell to send you off in the right direction.
Meg Thank you. Mog, Owl, come along.

They prepare to go. Meg and Mog board the broomstick. Mog holds on to the cauldron. Owl stands nearby

Eerie music

The Witches surround Meg, Mog and Owl and raise their broomsticks. They move round, incanting their spell

Meg, Mog and Owl could go round in the other direction, inside the Witches' circle

Witches Through fair or foul
Whatever the weather
Take Meg, Mog and Owl
To find their feather!

The Witches close in on Meg, Mog and Owl

Ab-ra-cad-ab-ra!

There is a flash and a puff of smoke, accompanied by whooshing noises

The Witches step back to reveal that Meg, Mog and Owl have disappeared. (In the original production this was achieved by the Witches travelling from side to side of the stage during the word "Abracadabra". Meg, Mog and Owl, masked by the witches, slipped into the wings one by one. By the end of the word, the Witches were centre stage again, with Meg, Mog and Owl safely "vanished")

The Lighting changes as the scene change begins

The Witches engineer the scene change. They either make it all happen as if by magic—for instance, with scenery flying in and out, or simply change the set themselves. It is suggested that Tess should be the "Stage Manager"

First the tree goes, to be replaced by a practical portcullis, hung between two crenellated walls, each wide enough for two actors to hide behind. The portcullis should be able to rise and fall

A small staircase could be set against one wall. Downstage is set a chest, suitable for three people to sit on

As the scene change ends, the Witches disappear, and we should feel that they have engineered the journey of Meg, Mog and Owl to the castle

Meg, Mog and Owl enter upstage of the portcullis, "outside", as it were, the castle. They have left the cauldron offstage. Meg carries her broomstick

Scene 4

The Castle.
Eerie noises. Spooky lighting. Goose-pimply music

Meg, Mog and Owl peer nervously through the archway

Meg (*whispering*) Now whatever happens, stick together.

They tentatively start to walk through—under the portcullis, which is raised

As they walk through the portcullis starts to descend with an ominous clanking sound

The Audience may shout a warning. In any event, Meg, Mog and Owl react to the noise by stopping—right under the falling portcullis

In the nick of time they spot it, and jump backwards, out of the way

The portcullis stops, then raises itself

Intrigued, Meg, Mog and Owl try again. They gingerly walk forward; but as they get under the portcullis, it starts descending threateningly. Again the Audience may shout out

This time, Meg and Mog jump forward—*into the castle. Owl jumps backwards, as before; the portcullis crashes to the ground, leaving Owl stranded outside. He bobs around helplessly*

Meg and Mog, unaware of what has happened, tread gingerly on, exploring the castle. More eerie noises

The audience may shout that Owl has been shut out. In any event, Meg goes to grab his wing . . .

(*Whispering*) Owl, keep up. Don't lag behind. Owl! Owl!

She can't find his wing. She turns and realises what has happened

He's gone. Mog, Owl's gone.

Mog turns and sees Owl fluttering outside the portcullis. Mog points this out to Meg

Oh, no; what are you doing out there?

Owl starts to climb the portcullis—aiming to get over the top. When he is a few lattices up, Meg and Mog go to the portcullis to watch

Do be careful, Owl.

Suddenly, the portcullis lifts—with Owl hanging on to it. He waves his arms in panic. Exciting music

Meg registers horror as Mog quickly slips under the portcullis, and helps Owl down. He pushes him through the gap at the bottom

In the original production, it was found that it was impracticable for Owl to climb the portcullis. It proved acceptable for him to simply flutter helplessly behind it and, when the portcullis was lifted, to be wary of coming out! Mog went under and pushed Owl through the gap

The portcullis starts lowering itself. Mog is taken unawares

Mog—quick!

In the nick of time Mog squeezes under the descending portcullis

The three are reunited and prepare to search on

Now, stick together and look for the feather!

As they move off, they are stopped in their tracks by a startling sound. From offstage we hear mournful weeping

Owl Whooooo!

Meg, Mog and Owl freeze with fright as the weeping noise approaches. Meg looks off towards it. Then back to the others

Meg Quick, hide!

All run off in different directions. Then, after a few paces, they turn back, realising they should be sticking together. They all take hands and start off again—but again in different directions—and pull against each other. A very loud weeping noise frightens them into separating and hiding in different places

Sir George enters, weeping. He is a knight, but not in armour. He wears a chainmail suit and tabard-like garment in quartered red and white

Sir George goes to the portcullis, looks out, then sits down in despair on the chest

Meg, Mog and Owl realise, from their various vantage points, that this person is harmless. In step, they creep up to him. He doesn't see them

Sir George Ah, ah, ah . . .

Each "ah" builds up to a big wail; on each "ah" Meg, Mog and Owl take a step—the rhythm helps the humour. Just as they reach him . . .

Ahhhhhhhhhh!

Surprised by the force of the wail, Meg, Mog and Owl retreat

They try again

Ah, ah, ah . . .

They reach him

Meg Excuse me . . .
Sir George Aaaaaaaaaaaah!

They retreat again, then try a third time

Ah, ah, ah . . .
Meg Hallo!
Sir George Aaaaah!

He cuts short his wail as Meg, Mog and Owl stand their ground, and he notices them. He speaks with a pronounced lisp

Who are you, pray? Friends or foes?

Meg I beg your pardon?
Sir George Friends or foes?
Meg Friends. I'm Meg, this is Mog, and that's Owl.
Owl Whooo! Oooo!
Meg He's saying, "Who are *you*?"
Sir George (*tearfully*) Sir George.
Meg A knight! Sir George, is this your castle?
Sir George Yea and nay.
Meg How do you mean, yeah and nay?
Sir George Yea, 'tis my castle, but nay, 'twill not be soon, alas. (*He sobs again*).
Meg Why not?
Sir George Because, forsooth, Sir François desireth it.
Owl Whoo?
Sir George Sir François. The knight who liveth in yon castle next door. He hath challenged me to a jousting match.
Meg A jousting match. That'll be fun.
Sir George For me, 'twill be no fun. If I lose, he winneth my castle.
Meg You might er . . . winneth.
Sir George Not against Sir François. Nobody winneth against him. He is enormous strong and he loveth fighting. I hate fighting. I desire just to be friends. Not foes.

Mog starts miming that the three of them should support Sir George and help. He does a little shadow-boxing to show what he means

Meg What? (*Understanding*) Mog says, can we help?
Sir George That I doubt. Unless you desire Sir François to bully you also. Alas, I must go and ready myself.
Meg Sir George, may we look round your castle?
Sir George Certainly. Take no notice of the ghost . . .

Sir George leaves

Owl Whoooo?
Meg The ghost?

But Sir George has gone

Owl Ooooo!

Meg and Owl are nervous about the thought of a ghost. Mog looks around, interested

Meg He must have been joking, Mog. I'm sure there are no ghosts here.

Owl rubs his tummy

Owl Oo.
Meg What's the matter? Butterflies in your tummy?

Owl shakes his head and mimes eating

You're hungry?

Owl nods

Go and get your sandwiches then.

Owl shakes his head

No? Why not?

Owl mimes that he is nervous about the ghost

You're worried about the ghost?

Owl Oo!

Mog mimes that he will fetch the sandwiches

Meg Mog will go and get your sandwiches for you. Thank you, Mog.

Mog goes to the archway. Clanking noise as the portcullis rises for him.

Mog exits

(*Sitting on the chest*) That's better. Come on, Owl.

Owl looks warily around

You're not *still* worried about the ghost, are you?

Owl shakes his head, then nods it

Don't be silly. I told you, there's no ghost here. I'm sure of it.

At this moment, eerie music and lighting heralds the arrival of a ghost through the archway. It looms and lurks in typical ghostly fashion. It is, in fact, Mog, covered by the tablecloth

The Audience will probably shout a warning. Meg ignores it and carries on talking, ad-libbing if necessary

So you've nothing to worry about. (*Looking straight out front*) I won't see a ghost today. And neither will you.

By this time, the ghost has advanced upon Meg and Owl, and tapped Owl on the shoulder. He freezes with fright and eventually plucks up the nerve to turn

Owl sees the ghost, reacts and runs off

(*Waffling on*) Silly old Owl. I'll take care of you.

The ghost sits down next to her. Without turning, Meg puts her arm round it, thinking it is Owl

(*Comforting "Owl"*) You're quite safe. Nothing's going to . . . (*She strokes the Ghost's head. She stops in her tracks, realising the head doesn't feel like Owl's. She looks at the Audience as if to say* "Is something wrong?" *then slowly she turns—sees the ghost and* . . .) Aaaaaah!

Meg runs off (*the opposite side to the one Owl ran off*). *The ghost chases after her*

Owl enters nervously the other side. He looks around, faces offstage and starts tiptoeing backwards

Meg enters the other side, doing the same thing

They approach each other backwards, panto-style, and bump into each other. Both jump violently and run in a circle, meeting each other again

They relax, with relief, as the Ghost enters behind them, approaches, then throws its covering white tablecloth over them—revealing Mog, who shakes with laughter

Meg and Owl scrabble under the cloth, then realize what has happened. They turn on Mog

Mog! It was you all the time. Under our tablecloth. That wasn't funny. You frightened Owl out of his twits.

Owl Ooh! Ooh! (*He points to Meg*)

Meg Me? Oh no! I knew it was Mog all the time! (*To Mog*) Where are Owl's sandwiches?

Mog produces the sandwiches. They all sit down again. Owl starts eating a sandwich

Eerie music and noises, as a "real" Ghost enters from behind the archway, through the portcullis

The Audience will probably shout a warning

Meg, Mog and Owl register this, as the Ghost looms behind them. They mime to the Audience "Is there something behind us?" "Yes", *reply the Audience All together, Meg, Mog and Owl turn. In the nick of time, the Ghost pops behind one side of the archway*

Meg, Mog and Owl, seeing nothing, turn back as though the Audience were having them on. The Ghost immediately pops out again and waves cheekily. The Audience react

They turn again; the Ghost disappears; encouraged by the Audience they go up to the archway. As they look at the side the Ghost is supposedly behind, he pops out from behind the other *side (in fact another actor in an identical ghost costume)*

Fun as the Audience direct Meg, Mog and Owl the other way, followed by a comic routine in which the Ghost flits from one side to the other. Eventually they see it and are chased, but it (the other one) pops up ahead of them. Only one Ghost is visible at a time—it appears to magically disappear to reappear in another place. Strange lighting effects

Finally both *Ghosts appear from opposite sides, advancing on Meg, Mog and Owl, who react terrified and hide their heads in the chest*

Then a sudden loud fanfare rings out. The Ghosts react, rather as though dawn has broken and they must hide, and they exit

The portcullis flies in

The fanfare is announcing that the jousting is about to start. The Lighting returns to normal

Sir George enters on horseback (an over-the-shoulders hobby horse). He is in armour, complete with helmet with a red ostrich feather, and a lance. He is nervous

Meg, Mog and Owl approach

Meg Good luck, Sir George.
Sir George Thanks. 'Twill be necessary, methinks. Sir François is tough as a tree trunk and strong as an ox.

A sudden, ominous galloping noise is heard approaching. A cry of "whoa"; a whinny

The music builds up towards the entrance of Sir François. He is as big as possible, also in armour and on a hobby-horse. He speaks with a French accent and carries a lance. He enters, and stands outside the archway

Meg, Mog and Owl hide

Sir François, with one strong hand, raises the portcullis to a sufficient height to allow him to enter. Laughing menacingly, he enters and aims a provocative jab with his lance towards Sir George

Sir François (*booming*) Art thou ready, Sir George?
Sir George Aye, Sir François. As ready as I'll ever be.

Fanfare. Sir François trots downstage cackling menacingly. He stands opposite Sir George

Sir François We joust thrice. Two falls, a submission or a knockout to decide.
Sir George If thou sayest so.

Fanfare as they "present lances", then exit either side

Mog and Owl emerge and look off expectantly

Tension rumble. The sound of hooves approaching. They get louder

Sir George enters first, rather slowly, and, seeing (opposite) Sir François approaching, cowers in trepidation. Sir François enters

Sir François only has to gently prod Sir George to make him fall

Sir François Ha, ha, ha. One love!

Sir François exits the side opposite the one from which he entered

Meg Boooo!
Owl Whoooo!

Meg, Mog and Owl help Sir George up

Sir George exits the other side

Mog mimes that they should help somehow

Meg What? We should help?

Mog nods

But how?

Thundering hooves approach once more

Mog has a sudden idea and dashes out of the portcullis archway

As the hooves get louder, he comes back with Meg's broomstick. He hands it to her, then jumps over it

Jump the broomstick! Good idea!

Sir François enters. He cannot see the broomstick, but the horse can, rears up, and totters uncertainly. Whinnies and "whoas"

A breathless Sir George enters, hiding his eyes in terror. His lance happens to knock into the tottering Sir François, who falls

Sir George (*amazed*) One all.
Meg Hooray!

Sir François staggers up and both knights exit

One more fall to win, Sir George!

Mog mimes to Meg to make a spell

What? A spell? Do you think that's wise? What if it goes wrong?

Mog nods, indicating that there's not much time left

Thundering hooves begin. Owl points offstage, echoing the urgency

All right then. (*She takes the broomstick and waves it*)

Music

Give poor Sir George
A better chance—
Make Sir François
Drop his lance.

The hooves get louder, and the knights enter

Suddenly Sir François stops dead and he and his horse go into a jaunty waltz. He cannot control himself and spins round, bemused

Sir George stops and watches, amazed

Meg, Mog and Owl, disbelieving, cluster together. Suddenly Meg realizes what has happened

(*Looking heavenwards, shouting*) I said "drop his lance", not "stop and dance"! Oh dear.

The music gets more frantic. Sir François' dancing is forced to become more energetic

Suddenly his horse heads for the portcullis. With a hideous "clunk" sound, Sir

François' head meets the bottom of the portcullis. Dazed, he turns, and drops his lance

(*Pointing at the lance*) It worked after all!
Sir François I submit! Sir George is victorious.
Meg Hooray!
Owl Whooo!

Sir François turns to go, and hits his head again. Clunk. He staggers out

The portcullis lowers itself

Mog shakes Sir George by the hand. If necessary, Sir George removes his hobby-horse

Sir George Thank you! Thank you! My castle is saved! How can I repay you?

Owl points to the red ostrich feather on Sir George's helmet

Owl Oooo!
Meg You're right, Owl. Sir George, could we possibly have your red ostrich feather?
Sir George For what purpose?
Meg We're on a quest to find the ingredients for a spell to get rid of the Stegosaurus . . .
Sir George The Stegosaurus?
Meg Yeth—I mean yes. A red ostrich feather is the first ingredient.
Sir George (*handing it to them*) 'Tis yours.
Meg Thank you. (*She fixes it in her hat*) Ingredient number one!
Sir George What is ingredient number two?

Meg thinks. She has temporarily forgotten

Meg I've forgotten! (*To the Audience*) Can anyone remember?

The Audience hopefully remember that the next ingredient is the tooth of a tiger

(*To the Audience*) Thank you. (*To Sir George*) The tooth of a tiger.
Sir George A tooth, forsooth! Where will you discover that?
Meg I don't know. (*Taking in the Audience*) Where could we find a tiger?

The Audience suggest ideas. If someone says India or Africa, Meg suggests that it would be too hot there. Finally they get the answer—a zoo

A zoo? Of course! A zoo!

SONG 5: TO THE ZOO

Meg	To the zoo
Owl	Oo oo
Meg	To the zoo
Owl	Oo oo
Meg	To the zoo zoo zoo

Sir George Toodle oo
Owl Oo oo
Meg
Sir George } (*together*) To the zoo
Owl Oo oo
Meg
Sir George } (*together*) To the zoo
Owl Oo oo
Meg That's what we'll do
Meg
Sir George } (*together*) Go to
The zoo.

The verses can be sung by Meg and Sir George together, or the lines can be split up as required

Meg
Sir George } (*together*) There are
Cheetahs
Chinchillas
Anteaters
Gorillas
There are mammals
Such as camels
And a kangaroo or two
Moose
'N' mongoose
Mice 'n'
Bison
Surely there must be a tiger too.

To the zoo
(*plus Owl*) Oo oo
To the zoo
(*plus Owl*) Oo oo
To the zoo zoo zoo
Toodle oo
(*plus Owl*) Oo oo
To the zoo
(*plus Owl*) Oo oo
To the zoo
(*plus Owl*) Oo oo
Meg That's what we'll do
Meg
Sir George } (*together*) Go to
The zoo.

There are
Dingos
Koalas
Flamingos
Impalas
Geese and ganders

Giant pandas
And a cockatoo or two
Sharks
'N' aardvarks
Minks 'n'
Lynx 'n'
Surely there must be a tiger too.

To the zoo
(*plus Owl*) Oo oo
To the zoo
(*plus Owl*) Oo oo
To the zoo zoo zoo
Toodle oo
(*plus Owl*) Oo oo
To the zoo
(*plus Owl*) Oo oo
To the zoo
(*plus Owl*) Oo oo
Meg That's what we'll do
Meg } (*together*) Go to
Sir George } The zoo
Owl Oo!

The music continues as Meg prepares to say a spell to fly them to the zoo

Mog fetches the cauldron, then joins Meg on the broomstick

Sir George Farewell.
Meg Goodbye, Sir George. And thank you!

Music

Meg (*chanting*) For the tooth of a tiger—
Ingredient two—
Take Meg, Mog and Owl
To find a zoo!

Flash. Whooshing noises. Meg, Mog and Owl start to take off

Black-out

Scene 4A

The Flight to the Zoo

Meg and Mog, on the broomstick, and Owl, fly to the zoo

A shadow puppet sequence

Music and sound effects acompany the action

(*1*) *Meg, Mog and Owl fly across the screen*

(*2*) *Animals enter, one at a time. An elephant, a camel and a giraffe have the necessary clear features to be identifiable in silhouette. Appropriate sound effects accompany each animal*

(3) *With the animals still in view, Meg, Mog and Owl fly overhead. The animals look up in surprise*

(4) *Meg, Mog and Owl hover above. Meg tries to control her frisky broomstick in order to land*

(5) *In an ungainly fashion, Meg, Mog and Owl descend. The animals scatter*

(6) *Meg, Mog and Owl disappear from the bottom of the frame*

Black-out

The whooshing sound of their descent is followed by a loud crash

During the black-out and the sound effect, the screen flies out. As quickly as possible, lights up on . . .

Scene 5

The Zoo

Meg, Mog and Owl recover from their undignified landing

The Zoo consists of two cut-out cages. One cage (in which the tiger lives) should have a practical door with a lock. It is important that the tiger cage is not labelled, because the Audience may try to tell Meg too soon

Meg Is this the zoo?
Owl (*nodding*) Whooo!
Meg Right. Tiger hunt. We'll look in all the cages till we find one. Mog go that way. Owl that way. Good luck.

Mog and Owl exit in opposite directions

Meg sticks her broomstick in the cauldron (it should be able to stand upright, leaning against the side, the brush part uppermost) and goes towards a cage

As she moves, a loud trumpeting sound comes from offstage, followed by a voice

Zookeeper (*off*) Now stand still, there's a good girl.

Trumpeting. Meg goes over in the direction of the noise

Stand *still*!
Meg (*calling*) Excuse me.

Trumpeting

Zookeeper (*off*) You're asking for trouble, you know, big trouble.

Trumpeting

Now don't be silly. Put me down! Put me down!

Meg (*calling*) Excuse me.

There is a crash

Zookeeper (*off*) Ow. That wasn't funny.

Trumpeting

Now stay there.

The Zookeeper enters. He looks ruffled. He wears very heavy spectacles, wellington boots and a butcher's apron with pockets. He carries a scrubbing brush

(*Abruptly*) What is it? We're closed.
Meg Sorry, but I wonder if you can help me?
Zookeeper I'm the one who needs help. Have you ever tried bathing an elephant?
Meg No.
Zookeeper It's no joke.

Trumpeting

(*Shouting off*) Quiet! (*To Meg*) Now, clear off. We're closed.
Meg But it's urgent.

As the Zookeeper talks, an elephant's trunk enters and grabs him round the waist

Zookeeper So is the elephant's bath ... Aaaaaaaah! (*He struggles with the trunk*) Let go! Aaaaaah!

Trumpeting. The Zookeeper struggles harder

There'll be no buns at bedtime.

Trumpeting

I mean it! (*To Meg*) Clear off. We're closed.

The Zookeeper is dragged offstage by the trunk

(*As he goes*) Aaaaaaah!

Meg shrugs her shoulders and takes off her hat

She returns to the cauldron and balances her hat on the broomstick, making it look like a scarecrow

From offstage more trumpeting noises ensue

Zookeeper (*off*) Now settle down, Emily, please. You've got to have a bath. Good girl.

Meg decides to explore. She wanders offstage

Suddenly, from offstage ...

Stay, Stay!

Struggling noises—the rattling of bars

No, don't sit down. Please . . .

More struggling noises, and a crash—the sound of breaking glass

Oh no! You've broken them. You can go without buns for a week.

Trumpeting remonstrations

They were my only pair.

The Zookeeper enters, holding his shattered spectacles

(*Shouting off*) They're ruined. And I can hardly see a thing without them . . . (*He turns and sees the "scarecrow"—Meg's hat on the broomstick*) Are you still here? I thought I told you to clear off. (*Advancing*) Go on. Scram. (*Quite near*) Are you listening to me? Scarper. Vamoose. (*Very near*) Go away. Shoo. Shoo.

Meg has wandered back in, and watches this

Meg What are you doing?
Zookeeper You keep out of this. Shoo, Shoo. (*He stops suddenly, looks from the Scarecrow to Meg, and pauses*) What's going on?

The Zookeeper prods Meg. Then he prods the hat and broomstick, which topple over

Aaaaaah! (*Realizing*) I'm sorry. I thought . . . The elephant sat on me specs, you see, and I'm lost without them.
Meg Oh dear. I am sorry. I was hoping you could help me.
Zookeeper How did you get in? The gate's locked.
Meg I flew.
Zookeeper Flew?
Meg I'm a witch.
Zookeeper A what?
Meg No, a witch.
Zookeeper A witch. Good gracious. I've never met a witch before. What do you want?
Meg I'm looking for a tiger.
Zookeeper Why, have you lost one?
Meg No, no. I'm interested to see one. If you've got such a thing. Please.
Zookeeper Well. All right, then. He's in there. (*He points her towards the tiger cage*) He's called Stripey.

Meg sets off with eagerness. The Zookeeper stops her in her tracks

But be careful. Dangerous animals, tigers.

Meg creeps to the cage. She peers in

Meg I can't see him.
Zookeeper He's probably asleep.
Meg He's not in there.

Zookeeper What do you mean, he's not in there? (*He peers into the cage*) He's . . .

Tension music as he registers concern, then gingerly goes to the cage door. He pushes it, it opens. He creeps inside. Then, suddenly . . .

He's not in there! He's escaped! Help! Don't panic! Sound the alarm! The Tiger's escaped! Stripey!

An alarm bell rings. A police siren sounds. The lighting flashes too, like a police car

Meg (*shouting*) Mog! Owl! Look out! The Tiger's escaped!

The Zookeeper and Meg rush around searching. They bump into each other

They exit in opposite directions

There is a babble of concerned animal noises

Mog enters

The alarm is still sounding, and the Zookeeper's voice can be heard, off

Zookeeper (*off*) Tiger alert! Danger! Wild animal on the loose! Stripey!

Mog looks nervous. Suddenly he sees Meg's hat, broomstick and cauldron. He picks up the hat and, fearing the worst, mimes his fear that Meg has been carried off by the Tiger

He looks out at the Audience, as if to ask where Meg is. The Audience hopefully point off in the direction Meg went. Mog starts to exit

The Zookeeper enters

(*calling*) Stripey! Where are you?

He sees Mog, and stops. The alarm stops ringing. Without his spectacles, the Zookeeper has to peer blindly

There you are! Come on, Stripey. Good cat. Good cat.

Mog, never having seen the Zookeeper before, is bemused, though not afraid. He shrugs and shakes his head. The Audience may shout out, but the Zookeeper continues his advance

No-one's going to hurt you. (*He makes friendly "Puss, Puss, Puss" noises*) Come on. You're just a great, big, soppy pussycat, aren't you?

Mog starts backing away from the advancing Zookeeper

That's it. Good boy, good boy.

Mog backs into the open door of the tiger cage

Yes, yes. That's it. Good cat! (*He slams the door, and locks it*) (*With a change of tone*) Gotcha. And never try to escape again. I'll get you something to eat, though you don't deserve it.

He stomps off, maybe bumping into something en route

Mog, frightened, tries to get out of the cage, darting along the bars

Meg enters

Meg (*calling*) Owl! Mog! Where are you?

The Audience will probably inform Meg where Mog is. In any event, Meg suddenly sees him in the cage

Mog! Come out! (*She tries the door*) It's locked! How did you get in there?

Mog mimes that he was put in. Meg gets the Audience to interpret

What's he saying? The Zookeeper put him in? He thought he was the Tiger? Of course! The elephant broke his specs; he saw your stripes, Mog, and mistook you for the Tiger! (*To the Audience*) Right?

Audience Yes.

Meg What are we going to do?

Mog mimes "a spell"

Do a spell?

Mog nods

To get you out?

Mog nods

Tell you what. I'll go one better. I'll do a transposition spell.

Mog cocks his head, as if to say "what?"

A transposition—a changing places spell. I'll make you change places with the Tiger. So the Tiger will end up in the cage, safe and sound.

Mog mimes indignantly—"What about me?"

What about you? Well, you will find yourself wherever the Tiger is *now*, and sniff your way back here. Right?

Mog isn't sure

Come on, Mog. We've got to find that Tiger for the second getting-rid-of-Steggy ingredient. This is a perfect method. Agree?

Mog nods, warily

Good. Stand by. (*She goes to the cauldron, puts her hat on, and concentrates*)

Music

As Meg chants the spell, she "produces" the ingredients and throws them in the cauldron. (She could either do this magically or simply take them from a pocket.) Then she waves her broomstick over the cauldron

(*chanting*)
Feather of raven
Leg of a frog
Make the Tiger
Swap with Mog!

Flash. Quick black-out. Two whooshing sounds to suggest the transposition

When the lights come up, Mog has disappeared. Owl is in the cage

Meg doesn't look at first

Meg (*to the Audience*) It's worked. I've done it! I've got a spell right!

The Audience shout out that she hasn't

I have! You don't understand! Mog's changed places with the Tiger. The Tiger's in the cage!

She indicates the cage. The Audience shouts out her mistake

But look, there's the Tig . . . (*She turns and does an enormous double take*) Aaaaaaaah! It's Owl. What are *you* doing in there?

Owl Whoo! Whoo!

Meg Oh, I don't think I'll ever get a spell right. (*She rushes to the cage*)

The Zookeeper enters with a bucket of tiger food

Zookeeper Here you are, Stripey. Come and get it! (*He sees Owl*) Who are you?

Meg (*embarrassed*) He's Owl.

Zookeeper Where's my Tiger?

Meg I don't know.

Zookeeper He was in there!

Meg No he wasn't!

Zookeeper He was. I caught him.

Meg No, you didn't. That was Mog.

Zookeeper Mog?

Meg My cat. Look, here he is!

Mog enters, dazed. He joins the group

Zookeeper But what's that Owl doing in the cage?

Meg I magicked him there. By mistake. Instead of your Tiger.

Zookeeper (*furiously*) So where's my Tiger?

Meg I don't know!

The Zookeeper unlocks the cage, leaving the key in the lock

Zookeeper Owl. Out!

Owl emerges. Meg and Mog greet him

Meg Owl. I'm sorry.

Zookeeper (*calling*) Stripey! Stripey!

The Zookeeper exits

Meg Maybe I should have used wing of bat instead of leg of frog. (*To Owl*) Are you all right?

Meg tries to comfort Owl

The Tiger enters. He is a Tiger-like version of an Indian Army Officer. He wears a topi, striped tiger-like combinations, army boots and medals. He has a moustache, sideburns and, of course, a tail

The Tiger stops suddenly when he sees Meg, Mog and Owl, who do not see him. He smiles

Tension music as the Tiger, licking his lips, stalks his way menacingly towards Meg, Mog and Owl, who still do not see him; they are busy being excitedly reunited

The Audience hopefully shout out a warning. As the Tiger prepares to spring. . .

the CURTAIN *falls*

ACT II

Scene 1

The Zoo

The play picks up where it left off. In fact, in the original production, the action started twenty seconds or so before the end of Act I—in other words, the final moments of Act I were repeated, in order to re-establish the situation

The Tiger, menacingly stalking, approaches Meg, Mog and Owl, who are not aware of him

Tension music

The Audience shouts out a warning

Mog suddenly sees the Tiger and mimes to the others to turn round. They leap with surprise and shock, then back away

The Tiger starts to chase them. Enjoyment rather than sheer menace should be his feeling, paving the way for later developments! Meg, Mog and Owl, however, see only danger, and back round in an effort to escape

Suddenly they all chase off, pursued by the Tiger. They go off the side the Tiger entered from at the end of Act I

The moment they exit, from the other side the Zookeeper enters, carrying the tiger food

Zookeeper (*calling*) Stripey! Stripey! (*He reaches centre, and calls out front*) Stripey! Where are you?

The Audience probably shout that he has gone off "that way"

That way? Thank you.

Unseen by the Zookeeper, the chase returns—behind him—and the Tiger chases Meg, Mog and Owl off the other side

The Zookeeper, following the instructions of the Audience, starts to exit the, now, wrong side

The Audience tell him he is going the wrong way. He stops

What? (*Wandering back to* C) *That* way? Are you sure?

Suddenly the chase returns, behind him as before, and exits the other side. The Audience indicate that side

Well, make your minds up! That way?

The Zookeeper exits that side

Upstage, Meg, Mog and Owl enter. Mog, thinking quickly, leads the others into the Tiger cage to hide

The Tiger enters. He doesn't see Meg, Mog and Owl in the cage, and exits the other side

So now the Tiger is offstage the opposite side from the Zookeeper

Meg, Mog and Owl emerge from the cage

Meg Oh dear, what are we going to do?

Mog has an idea. He mimes towards the cage, then points off in the Tiger's direction

The cage? What about it? Get the Tiger into the cage? Good idea. How can we do that? (*Thinking aloud out front*) What would tempt the Tiger back into his cage?

Hopefully the Audience shout out "food!" Mog nods agreement

Food? Yes, but we haven't got any food.

Suddenly Owl jumps about in excitement. He rushes to the cauldron and takes out the sandwiches. He holds them up

What? Your sandwiches? Do you think tigers like sandwiches? Well, it's worth a try. Quick. Put them in the cage.

Owl dithers in excitement

Quickly, Owl. In the cage. In the cage.

Owl goes in the cage and stands there holding out his sandwiches

(*to Mog*) We'll hide over there. (*Looking round for Owl*) Owl! *You* don't stay in the cage—just the sandwiches.

Owl leaves the cage, turns and holds the sandwiches inside

Put them down!
Owl Oo! (*He puts the sandwiches down*)

All three hide

The Tiger enters

Tension music

The Tiger excitedly prepares for another chase

Mog, thinking quickly, grabs the tablecloth from the cauldron. He spreads it out, and uses it like a bullfighter's cape, encouraging the Tiger to charge. Appropriate music

The Tiger likes the idea, and charges. Mog neatly sidesteps, letting the Tiger charge through

Same thing in the other direction. Charge. Sidestep. Meg and Owl watch from hiding

The third time, Mog manages to angle the tablecloth in such a way that the course of the Tiger's charge takes him to the cage. He charges, stops by the cage, and sniffs

Mog hides

The Tiger sniffs again. Then he speaks. He has a full-blooded "elderly Colonel"-type of voice. He is clearly a Tiger with Indian Raj background

Tiger Mmmm. Something smells rather special. I say! (*He sniffs again*) Mmmm. Terribly tasty, fearfully flavoursome, and exceedingly eatable! Peanut butter? Or is it anchovy paste? Much more appetizing than the familiar feeding-time fare! Worth investigation and no mistake. I wonder where it is . . .?

He sniffs around. The Audience hopefully encourage him to go in the cage. Eventually he sees the sandwiches

Bingo! (*He hesitates. To the Audience*) I say, this isn't a trick, is it?
Audience No.
Tiger It isn't a dastardly tiger trap?
Audience No.
Tiger Right, then. Here goes. (*He enters the cage and starts munching a sandwich*) Mmm. Delicious.

Meg, Mog and Owl dash out. Meg slams the cage door shut and turns the key

Meg Gotcha!
Tiger What? (*Realizing*) It *was* a tiger trap. (*Suddenly laughing*) Oh, well played! Fooled me fair and square! Ha, ha, ha.
Meg (*surprised*) Aren't you annoyed? Being locked up again?
Tiger No, no. I like it here. First class service. Lots of visitors. Ideal home for a retired tiger.
Meg Retired? You don't look old enough to be retired.
Tiger You're too kind. I'm still fairly frisky when given the chance! Which reminds me, thank you for that lovely game.
Meg Game?
Tiger All that chasing about. Splendid sport. Haven't enjoyed myself so much for years. Jolly decent of you.
Meg We didn't realize it was a game—we were terrified!
Owl Ooooooh!
Tiger Terrified? Of yours truly?
Meg Yes. Tigers are . . . well, not noted for being cuddly.
Tiger There's no need to be frightened of me . . .

SONG 6: LONG IN THE TOOTH

(*Singing*) When I reached retirement age
And found myself inside this cage

My life commenced a second stage
And all my anger and my rage
Seemed to gently disappear:
For though it may seem queer
I'm quite contented here——

I'm
Long in the tooth
Past my prime
Said goodbye to my youth
A long long time
Ago
Maybe I'm lazy
Maybe I'm a bore
But really I don't want to be
Ferocious any more.

During the next verse, Meg may let the Tiger out to do a soft shoe routine!

For
I'm
Long in the tooth
Past my prime
Said goodbye to my youth
A long long time
Ago
Maybe I'm crazy
Maybe I don't try
But really I would rather sit
And watch the world go by.

The tempo changes, and Meg, Mog and Owl temporarily take cover

When I was young
In the jungle
Life was diff'rent
I'd run and bounce
And leap and pounce
And spring to the attack.
When I was young
In the jungle
I joined the tiger cubs
And grew up to be
The leader of the pack.

He reassures them again

But now you must agree
I'm as harmless as a flea
You see

Meg and Owl could join in to "ooh" if required. During the last verse, the Tiger happily returns in his cage and Meg locks the door

I'm
Long in the tooth
Past my prime
Said goodbye to my youth
A long, long time
Ago
Maybe I'm lazy
Maybe I'm a bore
But really I don't want to be
Ferocious any more
I'm sure
It's unnatural
I'm sure
It's quite atrocious—
But really I don't want to be
Ferocious any more.

(*Speaking*) So, you see, you've nothing to fear. Long in the tooth, that's me.

Owl bobs up and down miming "tooth"

Owl Whoo! Whoo!
Meg What? Oh, yes! (*To the Tiger*) Er . . . talking of teeth . . .
Tiger What teeth?
Meg Your teeth.
Tiger Oh! Ha, ha, ha, ha! I'm so ancient, all my teeth have dropped out!
Meg You mean you're a toothless Tiger?
Tiger Exactly. Long in the tooth, short in the teeth! Ha, ha, ha.
Meg Oh dear.
Tiger Doesn't worry me. Saves cleaning them.
Meg No I mean "oh dear, we were hoping you could help us".
Tiger How?
Meg We're looking for a tiger's tooth. For a special spell to get rid of the Stegosaurus.
Tiger Sounds a shifty sort of blighter.
Meg He's a monster. He's gobbling up my garden. Gorging himself on my geraniums.
Tiger Mmm. Listen. My very last tooth only dropped out yesterday . . .
Owl Oooooh!

Mog mimes "where is it?"

Meg Mog's saying "Where is it?"
Tiger Under my pillow. Waiting for the fairies to collect it.
Meg Do you think I could have it?
Tiger Are you a fairy?
Meg Well, no. But I am a witch.
Tiger The fairies always leave ten p.
Meg (*thinking quickly*) Witches leave eleven p.
Tiger Fair enough. If it's still there, you shall have it.

Meg Thank you.

The Tiger exits to look

Tiger (*off*) Bingo!

He returns, with the tooth

Here it is.

He gives the tooth to Meg. Meg gives him money, which he examines with great pleasure

Meg Thank you! (*To the others*) Ingredient number two! (*She carefully puts it in her pocket*)

The Zookeeper enters, carrying the tiger food

Zookeeper (*calling*) Stripey! Stripey!
Meg It's all right, Zookeeper. We've found him.

The Zookeeper turns and sees the Tiger waving to him

Zookeeper Really? (*He shortsightedly goes to the cage, bumping into it on arrival*) Stripey, is that you?

The Tiger nods

It is! You're a naughty boy, but I'm glad to see you. Here's a bite to eat. (*He unlocks the door and enters the cage, to leave the tiger food*)

The Tiger briefly pops out again, unseen by the Zookeeper

Tiger (*to Meg, Mog and Owl*) See what I mean? Friendly staff! First class service!

The Tiger pops back into the cage, still unseen by the Zookeeper

Zookeeper (*leaving the cage*) Thank you all so much for finding him. Any time I can be of help, just give me a call, eh?
Meg We will.

Mog gets Meg's attention

What?

Mog mimes that they should be going

Ah yes. It's time to be off.
Zookeeper Where are you going?
Meg Wherever we can find our third ingredient ... the ... er ... I've forgotten what it is! Anyone remember?

Hopefully the Audience shout out "a cup of moondust". If not, Mog mimes—pointing to the moon

Moondust, of course. Where do we find that?

The Audience, led by Mog, tell her

The moon. How do we get there?

The Audience may shout out suggestions

(*As appropriate*) We haven't got a spaceship or a rocket ... and the broomstick won't take us that far ...

Mog points to the cauldron

The cauldron? Use that as a spaceship?

Mog nods, and runs to fetch it

Well, it's worth a try. All aboard. Goodbye, Zookeeper, thank you.

Zookeeper My pleasure. Safe journey. (*He stays to watch them go*)

Meg, Mog and Owl climb in the cauldron. Music

Meg chants a spell. Magic lighting

Meg
Cauldron, carry us up high
Like a spaceship through the sky
To the moon by magic spell
Stand by for countdown, earth farewell!

The Audience should join in the countdown

Ten, nine, eight, seven, six, five, four, three, two, one—LIFT-OFF!

Flash. Smoke. Loud whooshing noise

The cauldron rises

(*In the original production, Meg, Mog and Owl pulled the cauldron up around them like a huge lifebelt. It had a skirt of fluorescent flames attached, which hung down to conceal the characters' legs and show up against the black curtains, which flew in for a black theatre sequence*)

The Tiger and the Zookeeper wave goodbye

Lift-off! We have lift-off! Wheeeee!

SCENE 1A

The Flight to the Moon

SONG 7: DAY TRIP TO THE MOON

(*N.B. This song is sung offstage, or pre-recorded. It acts as a musical backing for the journey to the moon*)

Meg and Mog and Owl are flying to the moon
See it on the skyline hanging like a big balloon
Up among the stars

The Milky Way and Mars
Meg and Mog and Owl on a day trip to the moon
Away, away on a
Day trip to the moon.

Operation moondust, supersonic flight
Climbing in a cauldron quicker than the speed of light
Up and up they race
Way out in outer space
Meg and Mog and Owl on a day trip to the moon
Away, away on a
Day trip to the moon.

Looking at the lunar landscape drawing near
Standing by for landing, Meg and Mog and Owl are here
Time to go sightseeing,
Then fly home for tea
Meg and Mog and Owl on a day trip to the moon
Away, away on a
Day trip to the moon
Away, away on a
Day trip to the moon
Away, away
To the moon
Away, away
To the moon
Away, away
To the moon.

During the song, Meg, Mog and Owl, in the cauldron, fly to the moon

The method used to achieve this will clearly vary from production to production, depending on the technical facilities available

In the original production, the sequence was presented in U.V. lighting, in front of black curtains, to which were attached yellow stars, which shone out well. Meg, Mog and Owl, in the cauldron, "travelled", while various signs of the zodiac—Leo the Lion, Capricorn the Goat, Pisces the Fish and Cancer the Crab—passed them in the "sky". These were cut-out shapes, painted with fluorescent colour, operated by actors dressed all in black

Towards the end of the song the black curtains flew out to reveal the moon setting for Scene 2. Meg, Mog and Owl "landed" and started their scene on the moon

Or the sequence could take place inside the cauldron. *In other words, Meg, Mog and Owl—as well as the sky—could be seen from a cut-out "section". Through the "top" of the cauldron various heavenly bodies, stars, etc., could pass as the cauldron makes its way to the moon*

It would undoubtedly be most effective if Meg, Mog and Owl, in the cauldron, could actually rise and travel through the air

Whatever method is used, eventually the cauldron should land on the moon

Scene 2

The Moon

This scene is all done as a stylized mime, in which the movement skills of the actors convey the atmosphere of moon-walking

Exciting electronic music (based on the theme of Song 8) accompanies the whole scene

The following is a skeleton plan of events. Depending on the style of performance preferred, extra ideas may well be thought appropriate

(1) Meg, Mog and Owl climb out of the cauldron, and begin walking in an exaggerated moonwalking style. Meg carries her broomstick. Meg, Mog and Owl look about them in wonder. They experience difficulty in standing up straight; this makes them bump into each other—in slow motion

(2) Mog indicates the ground—where the moondust is. Meg signals her comprehension. She has no cup, but takes off her hat. Owl takes it from her and holds it on the ground, while Meg hands Mog the broomstick and indicates that he should use it to sweep the moondust into her hat. Mog begins to do this while Meg looks around in wonder

(3) When Mog has swept up enough moondust (glitter), he hands back the broomstick to Meg and signals to Owl to return the hat to Meg also. Owl does so; meanwhile Mog sees something offstage and exits. Meg, absentmindedly, goes to put her hat on, sprinkling glittering moondust everywhere in the process. She mimes her apologies for being so silly

(4) Owl has an idea. He fetches the tablecloth from the cauldron and spreads it on the ground. Meg sweeps some moondust on to the tablecloth. Owl helps. Together they carefully tie the corners, forming a bag to keep the moondust safe. Meg takes the bag and steps forward, holding it up. She mouths the words: "ingredient number three!" Then she hands it to Owl who takes it to the cauldron

(5) Mog enters with a moon buggy he has found. Meg narrowly avoids being knocked over by it. Then either *all get in the moon buggy,* or *Mog drives and the others follow on foot*

(6) After a short journey, they find a spaceship. This is a simple cut-out

(N.B. In the original production, it was decided that the moon buggy should not be a vehicle, rather a vacuum. Therefore the spaceship was already in position when Meg, Mog and Owl arrived on the moon. Instead of Meg and Owl collecting the moondust in the tablecloth, Mog appeared with the moon buggy and hoovered up the moondust with it. A small bag of moondust was then carefully pocketed by Meg. Mog pushed the moon buggy off-stage, then they all saw the spaceship)

(7) Meg approaches it gingerly, and knocks three times on the side. Out steps an astronaut in full rig. He greets them, with a salute. Mog has returned in time to see him

(8) The astronaut mimes "are you hungry?" They nod. So he reveals, three "speech balloons", lettered in upper and lower case. In the original production these were hinged from the proscenium arch. Written on the "balloons" are:

(a) Fish fingers
(b) Hamburger
(c) Strawberries

The astronaut invites them to choose. Owl points to "Hamburger"; Mog points to "Fish fingers"; Meg points to "Strawberries". They watch in eager anticipation as the astronaut rummages in the spaceship and emerges with . . . three identical lunar food kits—plastic bags with straws. He hands them out. Meg, Mog and Owl look disappointed, but shrug their shoulders and suck their straws. Clearly the taste is good

(9) As they "eat", the astronaut takes out a starting handle and attaches it to the bottom of his spaceship. He cranks it once, twice, thrice. Nothing happens. He mimes his frustration to the others. He could open a panel on the side of the spaceship; under it a sign, if possible lit up in red, reads "fault". The astronaut mimes his despair—he will have to stay here, it seems

(10) Mog mimes an idea—why don't they give him a tow? He mimes a rope being tied to the cauldron and to the spaceship. The astronaut agrees. He produces a towrope from the spaceship, and he and Mog attach it to their respective craft. Meanwhile, Meg and Owl tidy away their food packs and collect the broomstick

(11) They all get aboard—Meg, Mog and Owl in the cauldron and the astronaut inside the spaceship. With her fingers, Meg mimes the countdown—from ten to "lift-off"

(12) Puff of smoke. The cauldron achieves lift-off and exits. The tow-rope tightens. The spaceship, using "black theatre" method, is lifted up and swivelled to a horizontal position, then carried off horizontally, as though being towed by the cauldron

Fade to black-out

Scene 2A

The Flight Home

A shadow puppet sequence

A screen should fly in as quickly as possible after the previous scene. The puppets might effectively be seen against exciting sci-fi projections

Electronic music as Meg, Mog and Owl, in the cauldron, fly slowly along

The tow rope pulls on the spaceship

When the two craft are clearly visible, voices are heard—distorted as though through a radio intercom

Meg (*VO*) Cauldron to spaceship. Stand by for spaceship release. Over.
Astronaut (*VO*) Spaceship to cauldron. Spaceship standing by for release. Over.
Meg (*VO*) Go!

The tow rope breaks away and the spaceship changes direction and exits

Astronaut (*VO*) Thank you! Over.
Meg (*VO*) Goodbyeeeeee! Over and out.

The cauldron exits, and then re-enters from the other side. As it reaches the centre . . .

Look Mog, look Owl. We're nearly home! There's our garden.
Owl (*VO*) Oooooh!
Meg (*VO*) Ready to land!

The cauldron descends and exits from the bottom of the screen

Black-out

Electronic "whooshing" noises increase, to suggest that the cauldron is approaching earth. It lands with a huge splash. This should be timed with the descent and disappearance from the screen of the shadow puppets

Scene 3

Meg's Garden

Since Stegosaurus has by now devoured the whole garden, the set is bare

Meg, Mog and Owl are discovered in a heap, as though the cauldron has landed. They each have a frond of pondweed wrapped around them

Meg Trust us to land in the pond.

All three get up and look around

Look at our lovely garden.

Mog and Owl scratch their heads and look around

Owl (*sadly*) Ooooh.
Meg Exactly. There's nothing left to look at. He's gobbled the lot. Flowers, vegetables, trees, the lot. Oooooh!

Mog gets Meg's attention

Mm?

Mog mimes "Where is he?"

Where is he? Steggy? Mm. I want to give him a piece of my mind.

Mog mimes towards the house

What? He might be in the house?

Mog mimes eating

He might be eating the furniture? Chewing the chairs and bedding the bite ... I mean biting the bed?

Mog nods

Come on, quick!

They all creep off towards the house

From offstage the other side we hear grunts and eating noises. Then a bloated version of the "Steggy Stegosaurus" song begins

SONG 7A: STEGGY STEGOSAURUS (*reprise*)

Stegosaurus(*off*) Yummy yummy yummy
Scrummy scrummy scrummy
Chewy gooey chewy
Slurp (*noise*)

Stegosaurus enters. He has grown even bigger than his last entrance. This is achieved by adding another actor as a further segment, pantomime horse-style

Munchy munchy munchy
Scrunchy scrunchy scrunchy
Icky licky icky sticky
Burp (*noise*)

I'm a
Steggy Stegosaurus
Ug ug yummy
I'm a Steggy Stegosaurus
Fill my tummy
I'm a prehistoric beast
And I'm greedy for a feast
Where's my breakfast?

During the last line of the song, Stegosaurus yawns, and starts to nod off. He then makes sleepy noises

Enter Meg, leading on Mog and Owl

Meg He's not in the house. He must have gone. We've lost him ...

The Audience will probably shout out that he's behind her. In any event ...

A sudden loud snore from Stegosaurus stops Meg, Mog and Owl in their tracks

They freeze and look out front, then turn slowly and see the relaxed, bloated Stegosaurus and react to him

Owl Ooooh! Ooooh!
Meg Aaaaaaaaaah! He's enormous!

The others try to shush her

Stegosaurus stirs . . .

Stegosaurus (*blearily*) Yummy, yummy, yum . . . yum . . .

His eyes open. He doesn't see the others

Owl suddenly starts hooting a lullaby, and miming "sleep". He is suggesting to Meg that they should try to sing Stegosaurus back to sleep

Mog understands, nods, and indicates the Audience

Meg understands

Meg (*to the Audience*) Would you help us please? Sing him back to sleep!

SONG 8: LULLABY

This is "rock-a-bye baby", sung to "ooh"; Owl starts it off, then Meg joins in. The Audience is encouraged to join in too

When the lullaby is underway, Stegosaurus gradually settles himself back to sleep

The lullaby continues as Meg, Mog and Owl quietly prepare the spell. Meg and Mog position the cauldron. From it Meg removes the broomstick and the moondust. She carefully gives the red ostrich feather to Owl to hold, hands the moondust to Mog and searches in her pocket for the tiger's tooth

All the while the "ooohing" chorus of the lullaby continues, with everyone casting backward glances to check that Stegosaurus is asleep

The lullaby finishes as Meg, Mog and Owl, each holding an ingredient, are ready to perform the spell

Meg (*whispering*) Ready?
Owl Oooh!

Mog nods

SONG 8A: THE SPELL (*reprise*)

As Meg sings, Meg, Mog and Owl put the ingredients in the cauldron. Mog holds the broomstick

Meg Take a red ostrich feather
And mix it together
With the tooth of a tiger—sharp and white
Then add a cup of moondust—sparkling bright

Mog hands Meg the broomstick

Stir the ingredients, stir them well
Close your eyes and whisper this secret spell——

Feather, tooth, moondust
Tickle, bite, sneeze
Be gone Stegosaurus
Gone with the breeze.

Big flash. Puff of smoke. Black-out. Noise

When the lights come up, Meg, Mog and Owl turn round in excited anticipation. But . . . Stegosaurus is still there. He snores loudly

Meg (*with a gasp*) He's still here!
Owl Ooooh!
Meg I can't even get *other* witches' spells right. What will Tess and Bess and Cress and Jess say? Oh dear.

During this last speech, the Zookeeper has popped up from the cauldron, looking rather bewildered

Mog and Owl notice him first and nudge Meg

Zookeeper Where am I?
Meg It's the Zookeeper! Hallo.
Zookeeper (*peering*) Who's that?
Meg Meg, the witch. Remember?
Zookeeper Oh yes. Good gracious.
Meg What are *you* doing here?
Zookeeper I'm not sure. One moment I was polishing the three-toed sloth's toenails, the next . . . just like magic.
Meg It *was* magic, I'm afraid. *My* magic, going wrong.
Zookeeper How do you mean?
Meg I was doing a getting-rid-of-Stegosaurus spell, and . . .
Zookeeper (*getting excited*) A Stegosaurus? Did you say a Stegosaurus?
Meg Yes.
Zookeeper That's an extremely rare variety of monster.
Meg The rarer the better, I'd say. It's devastated my garden, chrysanths to cabbages, rhubarb to radishes.
Zookeeper You mean it's still here? I've never seen a live one.
Meg This one's live all right.

Stegosaurus snores loudly

Mog and Owl point towards him

Meg He's asleep now. Do you want to see him?
Zookeeper Yes please.

Meg helps him out of the cauldron. He peers in the wrong direction

Meg Over there. (*She directs him*)

Zookeeper Oh, it's so frustrating not having my specs ... (*He gets very close, and looks through a magnifying glass*) My word, he looks healthy.
Meg He's full of all my fruit and veg, that's why.
Zookeeper A splendid specimen, I'd say.
Meg A greedy glutton, *I'd* say.
Zookeeper You mean you're not keen to keep him?
Meg Keep him? I'd do anything to get rid of him! In fact I have! Mog, Owl and I have been zooming all over the place—castle, zoo, even the moon—getting special ingredients. And after all that, the rotten magic didn't work.
Owl (*shaking his head*) Ooooh.
Zookeeper I think it did.
Meg Of course it didn't—he's still here!
Zookeeper But the magic brought *me* here. And, with your permission, I'd like to take Stegosaurus back to the zoo. He'd be a great attraction.
Meg Do you really mean that?
Zookeeper Yes. Folk would come from miles around to see him.
Meg No, I mean, do you really mean you'd take him away?
Zookeeper Certainly. I said I'd help you after you found Stripey, and here's my chance. (*He goes to Stegosaurus and starts prodding and tickling him*) Wake up, Steggy, good Steggy, come on, wakey wakey!

Mog and Owl look worried

Meg Do be careful.

Stegosaurus stirs. He grunts

Zookeeper That's it. Good.
Stegosaurus (*with a roar*) Yummy, yummy, where's my breakfast? (*He leaps up*) Where's my feast?
Zookeeper (*hanging on to him*) Come with me and you can have as much breakfast as you want.
Stegosaurus Scrummy, scrummy, where's my breakfast?

Meg, Mog and Owl cluster together, nervous

Zookeeper At my zoo. Come on. I'll look after you there.

Stegosaurus grunts and struggles. The Zookeeper calms him down by singing

SONG 8B: TO THE ZOO (*reprise*)

Zookeeper	To the zoo
(*plus* **Owl**)	Oo oo
	To the zoo
(*plus* **Owl**)	Oo oo
	To the zoo zoo zoo
Meg	Toodle oo
(*plus* **Owl**)	Oo oo

Meg
Zookeeper } (*together*) To the zoo
(*plus* **Owl**) Oo oo
To the zoo
(*plus* **Owl**) Oo oo
Zookeeper That's what we'll do
Go to
the zoo

Stegosaurus decides he likes the idea

Stegosaurus To the zoo?
(*plus* **Owl**) Oo oo
Zookeeper To the zoo
(*plus* **Owl**) Oo oo
Stegosaurus To the zoo zoo zoo
Toodle oo
(*plus* **Owl**) Oo oo
All To the zoo
(*plus* **Owl**) Oo oo
To the zoo
(*plus* **Owl**) Oo oo
Zookeeper
Stegosaurus } (*together*) That's what we'll do
All Go to
The Zoo.
Stegosaurus Toodle Oo!
Zookeeper Off we go.

Music as Stegosaurus is led happily off—towards the house

Meg (*suddenly*) Wait! The zoo's in *that* direction!
Zookeeper Oh. Sorry. I'm lost without my specs.
Meg Tell you what! I'll mend them for you. By magic.
Zookeeper Good gracious. Will you really?
Meg I'll have a try. I must get *one* spell right today.
Zookeeper I've got all the pieces. (*He hands them to her, in a bag or handkerchief*)

Music as Meg takes them and places them in the handkerchief, which is in fact a magic prop, with a false pocket

Meg (*chanting*) Tweezers and squeezers
Pinches and pecks
Abracadabra
Mend these old specs.

Flash. "Whooshing" noise. Quick black-out, if necessary

When the Lights come up, Meg shakes the handkerchief

Here you are!

But the pieces have vanished

But . . . oh dear . . . they've disappeared! I'm so sorry.

Mog and Owl suddenly start pointing at the Zookeeper

Owl Oooh! Whoo!
Meg What? (*She looks at the Zookeeper*)

The Zookeeper suddenly realizes he has his specs on—restored to one piece

Zookeeper You did it! Thank you. They're perfect.
Stegosaurus Yummy, yummy, where's my breakfast?
Zookeeper All right, Steggy. (*To Meg*) Thanks again. Bye!

Music as he confidently leads Stegosaurus off. This leads into . . .

SONG 9: I GOT A SPELL RIGHT

Meg

I did it! I did it!
Didn't you see?
I did it! I did it!
Clever old me!
With my magic passes
I mended his glasses
It worked like a dream
And so it would seem—

I got a spell right
I knew I could
I got a spell right
And I feel good.

I got a spell right
I've learnt my trade
I got a spell right
I've made the grade.

Suddenly I've found the secret of success, yes
Suddenly my spells don't end up in a mess, no
That's why I'm behaving in this raving kind of way
For I believe in miracles and one took place today

A sudden "whooshing" noise makes Meg, Mog and Owl look around

Tess enters, landing on her broomstick. Meg rushes to greet her

(*To Tess*)

I got a spell right
I knew I could
I got a spell right
And I feel good.

Another whoosh as Jess enters

(**Tess** to **Jess**) Meg got a spell right
She's learnt her trade
Meg got a spell right
She's made the grade.

Meg Suddenly I feel I'm standing ten feet tall, 'cos
Now I know that I can do it after all, no
Nothing's so embarrassing as spells that never work
So is it any wonder that I'm going quite berserk

Another whoosh as Cress and Bess enter

(*N.B. In the original production, Cress was doubling as the Zookeeper, and "her" entrance had to be delayed until the end of the song, in order to make the costume change possible*)

Tess and **Jess** (*to* **Cress** *and* **Bess**) Meg got a spell right
She's learnt her trade
Meg got a spell right
She's made the grade.

Now the Witches and Meg sing in counterpoint

Meg Suddenly I've found the secret of success, yes	**Witches** Meg got a spell right
Suddenly my spells don't end up in a mess, no	We knew she could
That's why I'm behaving in this raving kind of way	Meg got a spell right
For I believe in miracles and one took place today.	And she feels good.
Suddenly I feel I'm standing ten feet tall, 'cos	Meg got a spell right
Now I know that I can do it after all, no	She's learnt her trade
Nothing's so embarrassing as spells that never work	Meg got a spell right
So is it any wonder that I'm going quite berserk?	She's made the grade.

Meg I got a spell right
Witches You got a spell right
Meg/Witches I've/you've made the grade.

All the Witches cluster round Meg, cheering

Meg Thank you, witches! And welcome to my Spell Party.
Tess What sort of spells shall we do?
Jess Nice spells?
Cress Nasty spells?
Bess Naughty spells?
Meg Well, I really haven't had time to think ...

Owl interrupts

Owl Oooh! Oooh!
Meg Yes, Owl?

Owl points sadly around the garden

The garden? I know. It's in a dreadful state. It all looks dead as a dodo.

Mog jumps forward

Yes, Mog?

Mog mimes that all the Witches should magic the garden back to normal

Do a magic spell? *All* do a magic spell? To make the garden grow again?

Mog nods

Tess Mm. Tricky.
Jess Nature spells are always tricky.
Cress Mother Nature isn't fooled easily.
Bess Her laws are impossible to break.
Meg Oh well, we'll just have to wait for next Spring and hope everything grows again then.

Meg, Mog and Owl turn and walk sadly upstage

Tess Unless . . .
Jess Perhaps . . .
Cress Supposing . . .
Bess Maybe . . .
All Four Witches Are you thinking what I'm thinking? Yes!

Meg, Mog and Owl turn to listen

Tess All we have to do . . .
Jess . . . is make the garden think that Spring is here . . .
Cress . . . then take it by surprise . . .
Bess . . . with a spell . . .
All 4 . . . a *growing* spell!
Meg But how do we make the garden think it's Springtime?
Tess Well, it's looking so dead, it probably thinks it's wintertime now. . .
Jess So a little storm . . .
Cress Lightning, thunder . . .
Bess Then some rain . . .
Tess Followed by some wind to blow the clouds away . . .
Meg (*catching on*) Sunshine . . . insects . . . birds . . .

The Witches all make insect and bird noises

. . . the garden thinks it's Springtime . . .
All 4 Yes . . . and we cast the growing spell!
Meg But how are we going to make lightning and thunder and rain and . . .

Mog is leaping about

Mog's got an idea. Go on, Mog.

Mog indicates the Audience

What? Everybody could help? How?

Owl jumps up and down

Owl Ooooh! Ooooh! (*He points to the Audience*)
Meg What? They could all make Springtime noises? It's worth a try. What do you think, Witches?
Tess That might work. Let's have a practice. First, lightning ... I know if everyone claps, that might be like lightning. All together. After three. One, two, three.

The Audience claps

Just one clap each. Again. One, two, three.

The Audience claps

Excellent.
Jess Then the thunder! (*Having an idea*) Everyone stamp on the floor. Go!

The Audience stamps

Good! Thank you. Now try again. Very loud to begin with, then tailing away into the distance. Go.

She conducts the stamping

Perfect.
Cress What's next? Rain. Can you make rain noises? "Whoosh" or "pitter, patter, pitter, patter", or "splish, splash, splosh". Let's hear the rain. After three. One, two, three.

The Audience make rain noises

Once again. Let's start with a bit of drizzle and build it up to proper rain. One, two, three.

She conducts the rain

Lovely.
Bess Now the wind—to blow the clouds away and bring the sunshine. Let's have a good whistling wind. One, two, three.

The Audience make whistling wind noises

Good. Once more. Another gust. One, two, three.

Another blow

Brilliant.
Meg Now, Mog and Owl lead the insect and bird noises. Anything you like—bees, crickets, cuckoos ...
Owl (*counting them in*) Oo! Oo! Oo!

The Audience make bird and insect noises

Meg Thank you.
Tess And then Meg casts the growing spell.
Meg Me?
Tess Of course! It's your Spell Party.
Meg Thank you. Should we try it all through once again?
Tess All right. Ready, everybody? Lightning!

The Audience clap

Jess Thunder.

Jess conducts the Audience stamping

Cress Rain.

Cress conducts the Audience rain noises

Bess Wind.

The Audience whistles and blows

Meg Birds and insects.

The Audience do bird and insect noises, encouraged by Mog and Owl

N.B. Each noise could have an accompanying action, demonstrated by the Witches, followed by the Audience

Then I cast the growing spell! (*To the Witches and the Audience*) Shall we try it for real now?
Witches / **Audience** } (*together*) Yes.
Meg Good luck, everybody; don't forget, make my garden really think it's Springtime. Now, let's start with hush—the calm before the storm. (*She lets the Audience settle. Then she nods to Tess to start*)
Tess (*mouthing or whispering*) Lightning!

The Audience clap

Jess (*mouthing or whispering*) Thunder!

Jess conducts the thunder

The Lighting darkens

Cress (*mouthing or whispering*) Rain!

Cress conducts the rain

Bess (*mouthing or whispering*) Wind!

As the Audience whistle and blow, the Lighting brightens to suggest the sun coming out

Meg (*mouthing or whispering*) Birds and insects!

The Audience, encouraged by Mog and Owl, do insect and bird noises

Music

Meg steps forward. All the Witches cross their fingers

Meg (*chanting*)
Swallows and bluebells
And squawk of a crow
Mix with a rainbow
To make the seeds grow!

Meg waves her broomstick

There is an expectant hush

Nothing happens

Meg looks anxious, then turns to the Audience

Please. Will you all help me? Say the spell after me? Will you?
Audience Yes.

Meg leads the Audience. The other Witches join in too. Meg performs actions to accompany the words

Meg	Swallows and bluebells
All (*including the Audience*)	Swallows and bluebells
Meg	And squawk of a crow
All	And squawk of a crow
Meg	Mix with a rainbow
All	Mix with a rainbow
Meg	To make the seeds grow!
All	To make the seeds grow!

All five Witches wave their broomsticks

Music and exciting sounds as a transformation scene happens—as magically as possible

The characters watch in delight

The transformation should not be rushed. In the original production, there were three simple stages:

(1) Green spirals grew upwards from the floor

(2) A gauze lit up to reveal very big flowers

(3) More flowers on japanese fans unfolded from the proscenium arches. Each stage was accompanied by a lighting change

As a final "moment" all the Witches could produce "magic" bouquets (from the sleeves of their cloaks?)

The final picture is one of colour and life

Meg Thank you—(*taking in the Audience*) Thank you all—it worked!

Everyone cheers

SONG 9A: I GOT A SPELL RIGHT MEG, MOG AND OWL (*reprise*)

Meg (*taking in the Audience*) We got a spell right
I knew we could
Meg and **Witches** We got a spell right
And we feel good.

We got a spell right
We've learnt our trade
We got a spell right
We've made the grade.

The Witches "present" Meg, Mog and Owl

Witches Meg, Mog and Owl
Owl Whoo!
Witches My, what a day!
It's far too late
To celebrate
Time for us to fly away.

The music continues as Meg, Mog and Owl yawn. Their bed flies in, summoned by the Witches' broomsticks. Alternatively, the Witches could bring the bed on. Meg, Mog and Owl climb in. As they sing, the Witches creep towards the wings

Through thick or thin
Owl (*tiredly*) Whoo!
Witches Fair wind or foul
Such friends as these
One seldom sees
Meg

Meg drops her head, asleep

Mog

Mog drops his head, asleep

And Owl!
Owl (*yawning*) Whoo! (*He falls asleep*)

The Witches vanish

Final picture of Meg, Mog and Owl in bed, as they started Act I

Black-out

CURTAIN

FURNITURE AND PROPERTY LIST

See Author's and Designer's notes on setting and properties

ACT I

Scene 1

On stage: Cut-out window
Green cuckoo clock with telephone-receiver weights
Cut-out bed with pillow and quilt
Alarm clock
Meg's shoes by bed
Meg's cloak on bed
Meg's hat
Broomstick

Scene 2

On stage: Staircase
Cauldron

Off stage: Spider **(Stage Management)**
Nest **(Stage Management)**
Beetle **(Stage Management)**
Package—with sandwiches **(Owl)**
White cloth **(Owl)**

Scene 2a

Shadow puppets as described in script

Scene 3

On stage: Dark blue cyclorama with crescent moon and stars
Tree

Magic items: (In Witches' hats): cup, saucer **(Tess)**; teapot containing brew **(Jess)**; milk bottle or rubber glove **(Cress)**; Sugar **(Bess)**; Spoon **(Cress)**

Personal: All **Witches** have broomsticks

Scene 4

On stage: Portcullis between two walls
Staircase (optional)
Chest

Off stage: Tablecloth **(Meg)**
Sandwiches **(Meg)**
Hobby-horse **(Sir George)**
Hobby-horse **(Sir François)**
Lance **(Sir George)**
Lance **(Sir François)**

SCENE 5

On stage: Two cages—one with a practical door and key

Off stage: Scrubbing brush **(Zookeeper)**
Ingredients for spell **(Meg)**
Tiger food in bucket **(Zookeeper)**

Personal: **Zookeeper;** shattered spectacles

ACT II

SCENE 1

On stage: As for Act I, SCENE 5

Off stage: Tiger tooth **(Tiger)**

SCENE 2

Set: Moondust, rocket etc. (see text)

SCENE 3

On stage: Bare set

Set: Ingredients in cauldron

Personal: **Zookeeper:** magnifying glass, pieces of spectacles
Meg: handkerchief

LIGHTING PLOT

ACT I, SCENE 1

To open: Morning light

Cue 1	As **Meg** "fluences" clock *Light pulsates whilst spell is said*	(Page 2)

ACT I, SCENE 2

To open: Morning light

Cue 2	**Meg:** "Bring breakfast for three." *Flash, then black-out*	(Page 5)
Cue 3	After extraordinary noises *Lights up*	(Page 5)
Cue 4	As broomstick takes off *Black-out*	(Page 11)

ACT I, SCENE 2A

See script for shadow puppet sequence

ACT I, SCENE 3

To open: Lights up quickly

Cue 5	**Witches:** "Ab-ra-cad-ab-ra." *Flash*	(Page 21)
Cue 6	As Meg, Mog and Owl "disappear" *Lighting changes as scene changes*	(Page 21)

ACT I, SCENE 4

To open: "Spooky" lighting

Cue 7	**Meg:** "I'm sure of it." *Eerie lighting*	(Page 25)
Cue 8	As comic routine with ghosts takes place *Strange lighting effects*	(Page 26)
Cue 9	As Fanfare sounds *Lights back to normal*	(Page 26)
Cue 10	**Meg:** "To find a zoo." *Flash, then black-out*	(Page 31)

ACT I, SCENE 4A

Cue 11 Shadow puppet sequence ends (Page 32)
Black-out

ACT I, SCENE 5

Cue 12 As SCENE 5 starts (Page 32)
Lights up to exterior level

Cue 13 As police siren sounds (Page 35)
Lights flash like police car

Cue 14 **Meg:** "Swap with Mog!" (Page 37)
Flash. Black-out. Then lights up after whoosh

ACT II, SCENE 1

To open: Outdoor lighting

Cue 15 **Meg** chants spell (Page 45)
"Magic" lighting

Cue 16 **Meg:** "LIFT-OFF!" (Page 45)
Flash

Cue 17 See text for SCENE 1A

ACT II, SCENE 2

Cue 18 Lighting as required (Page 47)

ACT II, SCENE 2A

See script for shadow puppet sequence

ACT II, SCENE 3

To open: Outdoor lighting

Cue 19 **Meg:** "Gone with the breeze." (Page 52)
Flash then black-out. Then up to full

Cue 20 **Meg:** "Mend these old specs." (Page 54)
Flash, black-out, then up to full

Cue 21 Audience stamps for thunder (Page 59)
Lights darken

Cue 22 Audience whistles (Page 59)
Lights brighten

Cue 23 See text for transformation scene

Cue 24 Final "picture" (Page 61)
Black-out

EFFECTS PLOT

(see score for some scripted musical effects)

ACT I

Cue 1 As Curtain rises (Page 1)
Tick-tock of clock. Fade discreetly

Cue 2 After **Owl**'s third "oooo" (Page 1)
Alarm bell rings

Cue 3 **Meg** presses **Owl**'s nose (Page 1)
Hooter sounds

Cue 4 **Meg** presses **Owl**'s nose a second time (Page 1)
Hooter sounds

Cue 5 **Meg** presses **Owl**'s nose a third time (Page 1)
Hooter sounds

Cue 6 **Owl** switches off alarm (Page 1)
Alarm stops

Cue 7 **Meg:** "Bring breakfast for three." (Page 5)
Puff of smoke

Cue 8 In Black-out (Page 5)
Extraordinary noises

Cue 9 **Meg:** ". . . in the garden. He's . . ." (Page 7)
Crunching and biting

Cue 10 **Meg:** ". . . in my cabbage patch!" (Page 7)
Munching increases

Cue 11 **Steg** dashes off (Page 8)
Eating noises return

Cue 12 **Mog** nudges **Meg** (Page 8)
Eating noises continue

Cue 13 **Meg:** ". . . making-**Steggy**-*appear* spell." (Page 8)
Eating noises get louder

Cue 14 **Meg, Mog** and **Owl** look up the stairs (Page 9)
Whooshing sound

Cue 15 Broomstick takes off (Page 11)
Whooshing sound

Cue 16 In shadowplay as all four **Witches** take off (Page 12)
Whooshing sound

Cue 17 As **Meg, Mog** and **Owl** suddenly drop (Page 13)
Whooshing sound

Cue 18	**Meg, Mog** and **Owl** rise above **Witch** *Whoosh*	(Page 13)
Cue 19	In Black-out *Whoosh, then crash*	(Page 13)
Cue 20	As **Tess** enters *Whoosh*	(Page 13)
Cue 21	As **Cress** enters *Whoosh*	(Page 14)
Cue 22	As **Jess** enters *Whoosh*	(Page 14)
Cue 23	As **Bess** enters *Whoosh*	(Page 14)
Cue 24	**Witches:** "Ab-ra-cad-ab-ra." *Puff of smoke, whooshing*	(Page 21)
Cue 25	As portcullis starts to descend *Clanking*	(Page 22)
Cue 26	**Meg** and **Mog** explore castle *Eerie noises*	(Page 22)
Cue 27	**Mog** goes to portcullis *Clanking as portcullis rises*	(Page 25)
Cue 28	Both ghosts advance on **Meg** *Loud fanfare*	(Page 26)
Cue 29	**Sir George:** ". . . and strong as an ox." *Galloping noise and "Whoa"*	(Page 27)
Cue 30	**Sir George:** "as I'll ever be." *Fanfare*	(Page 27)
Cue 31	**Sir George** and **Sir François** present lances *Fanfare*	(Page 27)
Cue 32	Tension rumble from orchestra *Hooves approach*	(Page 27)
Cue 33	**Meg:** "But how?" *Thundering hooves, increasing in intensity*	(Page 28)
Cue 34	**Sir François'** horse rears *Whinnies*	(Page 28)
Cue 35	**Mog** indicates there is not much time *Thundering hooves, increasing*	(Page 28)
Cue 36	**Meg:** "To find a zoo!" *Whooshing*	(Page 31)
Cue 37	SCENE 4A (see text)	
Cue 38	In Black-out *Whoosh of descent, loud crash*	(Page 32)
Cue 39	**Meg** moves towards cage *Trumpeting sound, continuing as script*	(Page 32)

Cue 40	**Meg:** "Excuse me." (2nd time) *Crash*	(Page 33)
Cue 41	**Zookeeper** (*off*): "Stay. Stay." *Struggle noises, rattling of bars, crash of glass (see script)*	(Page 34)
Cue 42	**Zookeeper:** "The tiger's escaped! Stripey!" *Alarm bell (ring until scripted to stop), police siren*	(Page 35)
Cue 43	**Meg** and **Zookeeper** exit in opposite directions *Babble of animal sounds*	(Page 35)
Cue 44	**Meg:** "Swop with **Mog**!" *Two whooshes after Black-out*	(Page 37)

ACT II

Cue 45	**Meg:** "LIFT-OFF!" *Smoke, whooshing noise*	(Page 45)
Cue 46	See Scene 2a for effects	
Cue 47	**Meg, Mog** and **Owl** creep towards the house *Grunts and eating noises*	(Page 50)
Cue 48	**Meg:** "Gone with the breeze." *Puff of smoke*	(Page 52)
Cue 49	**Meg:** "Mend these specs." *Whooshing noises*	(Page 54)
Cue 50	**Meg** (*singing*): "... one took place today." *Whooshing*	(Page 55)
Cue 51	**Meg** (*singing*): "And I feel good." *Whoosh*	(Page 55)
Cue 52	**Meg** (*singing*): "I'm going quite berserk?" *Whoosh*	(Page 56)

www.ingramcontent.com/pod-product-compliance
Lightning Source LLC
LaVergne TN
LVHW051757080426
835511LV00018B/3343
* 9 7 8 0 5 7 3 0 5 0 6 5 7 *